WHEN WORK BECOMES OPTIONAL

WHEN WORK BECOMES OPTIONAL

Cheers.

Stan Corey

ISBN-13: 978-0-692-14752-8 (paperback)

Library of Congress Control Number: 2018907582

PRINTED IN THE USA

10 9 8 7 6 5 4 3 2 1

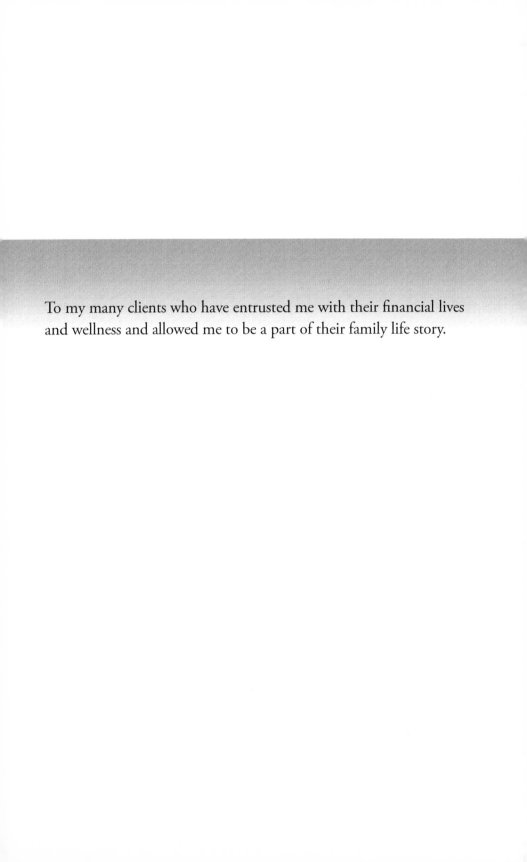

To my many clients who have entrusted me with their financial lives and wellness and allowed me to be a part of their family life story.

TABLE OF CONTENTS

PREFACE

IN 1964, BOB DYLAN wrote the song, "The Times They Are a-Changin'. " As he sang those famous words, I wonder if he had any idea how much they would come to represent an entire generation of Americans. No doubt, those born in the 1940s, 1950s, and 1960s have improved the world through championing civil and women's rights, the technological revolution, the redefinition of family and the workplace, and rock and roll. And their ability to shift paradigms continues as they influence what it means to retire.

Merriam-Webster defines retirement as "the state of being retired, withdrawal from one's position or occupation or from active working life." With all due respect to the famous dictionary publisher, one glaring problem I find with this definition is that retirement, in fact, no longer exists!

Working with clients as a financial advisor has shown me that the current generation of retirees is not following the path of their parents. Even the "r-word" (retirement) is problematic for many of them because it conjures up images of sitting in a rocking chair and staring out the window to the world beyond one's living room. Truth be told, retirement today bears little resemblance to *withdrawal* from active working life. Many of today's retirees have no intention of stopping and are seeking to live the rest of their lives with purpose and adventure. For them, this stage is not just a shift in living *but a shift in thinking as well.*

Based on these reasons, I offer a more relevant definition of retirement:

Retirement is when work becomes optional.

Making work optional may signal an end to one type of work: no more showing up to the office Monday through Friday and no more mandatory commutes and work travel. But, more meaningful to today's retirees, it signals a bright beginning: freedom to define work on your own terms and according to your own wishes. Who wouldn't be thrilled to embark on that kind of amazing journey?

For these financially savvy and motivated individuals, making work optional is less about asset accumulation and more about developing "emotional wealth," which is how to enhance our lives by doing good, following our own paths, continuing to learn, seeking new challenges, and exploring new opportunities to improve our own lives as well as the lives of those around us.

While making work optional is full of opportunity, like any major transition, this stage can be anxiety inducing as well. It can be a time to continue the work you've been performing, but possibly at a reduced pace. Or it can be a difficult period of letting go, as you release your hold on an identity that has been linked to the workplace your entire adult life. Or you may find yourself working into your seventies and beyond, perhaps because you're afraid of running out of money or maybe because you have a passion for what you've been doing and want to continue.

Whatever your circumstances, making work optional is less about a specific age and more about taking control of your life and physical and emotional wellness, maintaining financial independence, and pursuing your passions.

PART ONE
Setting the Stage

Why retire? If you're at this stage in your life, you've probably asked yourself this question. For many, they have no choice because their work requires them to retire by a specific age. This is the case for those working in law enforcement, in certain government agencies, as airline pilots, and in other occupations where the risk of having an older employee may endanger the people they are intended to serve.

For others, however, reaching normal retirement age sixty-five or deciding to retire earlier no longer has the same meaning it did a generation ago. Many of us feel we can continue to contribute, if not in our current occupation then in another role we find to be satisfying from a personal and an emotional standpoint.

Many professionals from doctors, lawyers, and professors to financial advisors and corporate executives have built their lives around working in their field of choice and cannot dream of doing anything else. That is why we are seeing so many more people continue their careers well into their seventies and even eighties. For many others, reaching a time when work becomes optional means having the freedom to try something new and different and following their passions without worry about the amount of income it generates. This can also be a time of stress if, in fact, you do need to continue working, as finding new work in your sixties can be challenging.

A key to a successful retirement is finding a new passion in your life. There is an old saying, "If it is going to be, it is up to me!" Retirement is a new awakening and a new opportunity to live the life you have always envisioned. So take charge and go for it!

CHAPTER 1
CRYSTAL BALL

"**S**TAN, CAN'T YOU JUST** peek into your crystal ball so you can answer my questions with 100 percent certainty?"

During my nearly forty-year career providing financial guidance and advisory services to individuals, couples, multi-generational families, and small businesses, I've heard variations on this question from my clients countless times. This is particularly the case when my clients are embarking on their "making work optional years," which is a time when people typically seek more security and predictability. For many, this often marks one of the biggest and scariest transitions they will ever experience in their lifetimes.

I've worked with clients who represent a wide range of experiences. Some have lived well into their nineties; others have passed away shortly after retirement; some have suffered the death of a spouse, sibling, child, or even a grandchild; some have divorced early in their careers or post-retirement; others have enjoyed retirement with the love of their life until the very end.

I've had the privilege of helping people transition from their working careers to retirement, manage their financial lives throughout, and pass down their legacy to the next generation. In regard to legacy, it isn't always only about leaving money behind. Often it comprises passing on a person's core principles and values.

Working closely with my clients, sometimes over decades, has given me deep insight into how people define this stage in their lives. Over the years, my clients have provided diverse definitions of retirement. The following is a sampling of what they've shared with me.

Retirement is:

- rewiring your life.

- having a plan and staying active.

- the moment in life you can finally make YOU the priority.

- building a sacred place to do something for your soul! It's time to reflect and give back to your community and the world. It's about connecting your soul to whatever higher being you believe in.

- not having to drag your butt out of bed at zero-dark-thirty!

- liberation from work and the opportunity to create and experience as many great moments as possible.

- a time to think and create new memories.

- when you have all day to do something and it takes all day to do it!

- not your end game.

- when you can pursue your passion on your own terms.

- time to take on new challenges, have new experiences, and enjoy family and friends.

- spending the rest of your life with those you love.

Do any of these resonate with you?

Based on these responses, retirement can be summed up as an emotionally charged period, and for good reason. No doubt, retirement is often associated with:

- doubts related to determining when or how to retire;

- anxiety about running out of money;

- fear over no longer receiving a paycheck or feeling guilty for not having one;

- worrying about how to stay active, mentally and physically;

- concerns about living too long;

- worries about the surviving spouse or other family members;

- uncertainty about how to navigate being part of the "sandwich generation," where one is charged to care for one's elderly parents as well as one's own children.

With the retirement stakes so high, no wonder the divorce rate among people in their sixties is rising! The good news is that it doesn't have to be this way. In fact, you can experience the opposite and have a thrilling stage of life where you are active, excited, and motivated to live in ways you have never done before.

WHERE DID ALL THE YEARS GO?

In his song, "He Went to Paris," Jimmy Buffet writes:

> *". . . some of it's magic, some of it's tragic*
> *But I had a good life all the way."*

If you're like me, when you look back on your life, you may find yourself wondering how time passed so quickly. In fact, it may seem that just yesterday, you were young and looking forward to your next adventure. I've been an avid sailor for most of life, so my adventures usually took place on the high seas. Now I am happy to simply mess about in boats!

Today, when you look into the mirror, perhaps you don't recognize the person you see. You may find yourself feeling younger than the image in the reflection. You may observe your friends and notice they are also graying and slowing down. Some have maintained good health, while others have not been as fortunate.

In my case, transitioning into retirement means I'm seeing more doctors in the past couple of years than I've visited in the past five decades combined. For example, every time I visit the dermatologist nowadays, she finds another little spot, stares at it, and says, "Hmmm. That looks interesting."

"I don't want to hear 'interesting.' I want to hear 'boring'" is my defiant reply.

She comforts me by telling me that for a sailor who spent decades directly in the sun as well as with its rays bouncing off the glassy waters below, I have much fewer suspicious spots on my face than she would have expected. I guess having a beard for twenty-five years provided more protection than sunscreen, which didn't exist in the 1960s and 1970s when I spent hours and days sailing along the Atlantic Coast.

"Wasn't life much simpler back then?" you may ask yourself—back when you were young and invincible and not worried about sunburn or wearing helmets to ride a bicycle. When hitchhiking to the next town or home from school after late sports practice or skipping lunch to go fishing or hunting seemed like great ideas.

I think about my mom and dad who, by today's standards of helicopter parenting, would have been thrown in the slammer for child neglect. The rules of the Corey household were simple: check in after school and then go play until dinnertime.

My siblings and I were rarely at home. Instead, we were outside running around the neighborhood, participating in pickup games of baseball, football, or basketball, hanging out at the creek, or in a friend's backyard. Little did we know then that those might have been some of the best days of our lives, ones we thought would go on forever!

Can you relate?

Through our social interaction, we learned how to make decisions, often through trial and error, and we had some control over our lives, took risks, and learned from our mistakes. One of the unknown questions of today is, Will all the controls and oversight placed upon children help or hurt them in the future when they are on their own?

Part of Einstein's theory of relativity explained that the faster you go in any one direction, the more time slows down. The inverse of that equation would be time accelerates as we age! For me, this means when I reflect on my life, the years have sped by, largely without my realizing it, until boom! I am facing the reality of retirement. I recently saw a woman wearing a T-shirt that said, "I know I'm getting older; I just didn't know it would come this fast."

POTENTIAL RETIREMENT PITFALLS

According to the United States Census Bureau, in 2016, over ten thousand baby boomers were retiring every day. For many, retirement is often the end goal. It's the reason they've invested countless hours commuting long hours to the office. But once they finally embark on this stage of their lives, I've observed that many suddenly realize retirement isn't the goal. Instead, it's just the fifty-yard line or half-time in their financial lives.

Think about so many men and women who, for their entire working lives, dreamed about reaching the ultimate goal of retirement only to find out it is far from a destination. Rather, it's the beginning of a whole new stage in life with new challenges and rewards.

Given that retirement means you have a new life ahead of you, living it well requires planning for it and regularly performing course corrections. Unless you actively plan, however, and focus on how you'll transition into retirement, you run the risk of being disappointed, if not downright depressed, during this stage of life that years ago may have seemed so magical.

As a result, thinking about the next fifty yards often creates anxiety. For many, the transition into retirement is one of the most challenging periods we'll ever face. It touches our emotions and finances. It forces us to think of our physical limitations and confront the big issue, our mortality. In addition, it may reflect our cultural biases.

First, there's the emotional part. Once you're retired, you're charged to reset routines you've maintained for decades, adopt a new lifestyle, and reevaluate your life. No longer is your calendar full of meetings, calls, and work travel. Instead, you fire up your laptop and see your corporate email account has been deleted. No one is requesting you to put out workplace fires or to meet with you. Now that you're gone, life has continued at the office, and you've lost contact with your colleagues and coworkers. As the days and weeks pass, you find yourself regularly asking at the top of each morning, "What am I going to do today?" (One of my retired friends referred to retirement as waking up and feeling each day was Saturday.)

You may fear you'll no longer command the same respect you did at your workplace. So instead of being the go-to person for answers and advice, you'll become irrelevant, like a flip-phone that was once the world's fastest and best but was instantly replaced by something even faster and better.

Once you retire from your position at work, you may wonder what to say when someone you just met asks, "So what do you do for a living?" To avoid this identity crisis, I recommend a simple step to take right away, while you're still working and haven't transitioned into retirement yet. Think about changing your answer from "I am a (fill in the blank with your title or position)" to the role you play in improving your organization or other people's lives. In my case, when I'm asked the question about what I do, I say, "I help people make better financial decisions," instead of, "I am a financial planner." It's an easy yet significant way to change your mindset.

Second, there's the financial part. Just thinking about the following three words may be enough to send you into a panic: *no more paychecks.*

You may worry whether you'll have enough savings to last your lifetime. You may wonder what would happen if you or your spouse had a major illness. Would it wipe out your nest egg? Or you may be concerned whether you'll have the funds necessary to leave a legacy to your family members and organizations you care about most.

Even people who have planned for retirement, spent their whole lives saving and investing, contributed to retirement plans, supported kids through college, and happily anticipated this moment in their lives often find themselves with retirement cold feet. In fact, I've observed a common thread most people who have thoroughly planned for retirement share: discomfort with the dramatic and sometimes scary shift from living on earned income to living on all they've saved for retirement. It is as if they need permission to spend what they have saved!

Third, there's the physical part, which addresses the reduction in our ability to be as mobile and as strong as we were maybe just a few years earlier. This may be the hardest part to envision when young. For example, when I was playing golf with my friend, who's retired and seventy-five years old, I asked him: "How do you explain the physical challenges of aging to the younger generation who are in their thirties and feel invincible (which is exactly how we felt when we were their age)?"

He answered, "When kids in their invincible twenties and thirties want to know what retirement's like, I give them my five-ingredient retirement recipe." My friend then described the following:

1. Wear three-pound ankle weights and one-pound wrist weights.

2. Strap ten pounds to your back.

3. Wrap each knee tightly with bulky ACE bandages, so you can barely bend your knees.

4. Put on golf gloves, and then try texting and opening tiny prescription pill bottles (of which you have a collection prescribed by your doctor).

5. Have smudged eyeglasses strapped to your face all day and cotton stuffed in your ears.

After hearing this, these young folk quickly get his point. From a physical perspective, retirement isn't easy. While my golf buddy's somewhat humorous description casts a sad shadow on retirement, the game itself provides fertile ground for entertaining and positive perspectives too. Here's an example: The older you get, the slower you swing. But the ball goes straight, maybe for the first time in your life—sometimes slowing down means progress!

This description brings me to my next point: Throughout your retirement, remember that a light heart and laughter will help keep you enjoying life. This means you try to not take yourself too seriously and to avoid hanging around negative people because they will drag you down with them.

Another reason why just the thought of retirement is cringe worthy may be cultural. In interviewing people who have migrated to the United States, many explained to me how their native countries valued their elders more than we do. This is particularly the case for parts of the developing world that place a high value on extended families and have not adopted the nuclear-family model on any wide scale.

In these parts of the world, multiple generations live in the same geographic area, if not under the same roof. At the household's hub is the patriarch or matriarch or both. This person's central role within the family means respecting one's elders is embedded within the culture. Elders' advanced age and wisdom are prized and often associated with a connection to a higher power deepened over a lifetime. No Botox or fillers for these old men and women. They proudly wear their wrinkles as badges of honor!

Communal meals may begin only after the elder takes a seat and eats the first bite. Younger family members may be required to use formal language and bow to demonstrate deference to their superiors, and the oldest family members may have the final say on others' major decisions such as marriage, finances, and business affairs. This type of communal culture contrasts with the US emphasis on the rugged individual.

Here in the United States, families are often scattered across our massive nation, each encouraged to fulfill his or her destiny. Grandparents,

parents, sons, daughters, aunts, and cousins may live multiple time zones apart or even in different areas of the world. Under these spread-out circumstances, families have, in general, evolved to not be required to provide caregiving services to one another.

And where a family caregiving tradition exists, the responsibility to look after parents and grandparents typically falls on wives and adult daughters. These women may live away from the older family members that require care. In addition, they're typically busy with full-time work and raising their own nuclear families.

Combined or individually, these two factors have created a dilemma for families as they figure out how to meet the needs of elderly parents or grandparents or both that can no longer take care of themselves. When multiple siblings are ostensibly charged to take on this responsibility, designating someone or stepping up yourself to do so can create conflict between brothers and sisters.

Within my financial practice, I've certainly witnessed my share of squabbles among clients over elder care with their family members. One aim of this book is to help you avoid such problems within your family. So, if you're the patriarch or matriarch who will require care later, I recommend you develop your own retirement living plans, rather than rely on the decisions other family members or even strangers will make on your behalf in the event you're unable to do so.

On the one hand, the emotional, financial, and physical challenges as well as cultural perspectives regarding retirement can easily result in an existential crisis as big as any other you've ever faced. On the other hand, many who reach this stage find themselves quite happy. Even if they do not have a large stash of cash or investments, they have figured out how to live off what they have, and they've chosen to not focus on what they don't have.

My research and experience has shown the people that have the greatest challenges at time of retirement are not the average blue-collar or middle white-collar employee. Rather, executives, professionals, and self-employed persons (both men and women) seem to face this stage of their lives with trepidation. In many cases, this is because these men and women have tied their identity to their work.

BIG QUESTIONS

As we summit the mountaintop we have spent our work lives climbing, we may find ourselves asking, "Where do we go from here? What decisions will make the difference for us to have the retirement we always dreamed about? What challenges lie ahead, and what will amaze us?"

In the final analysis, however, I've come to realize most client concerns boil down to answering the following question:

How do I maintain both financial and physical independence throughout my retirement life?

If this resonates with you, then you've come to right place! When my clients ask me to make predictions as far as their retirement is concerned, I often must break the news to them, "Unfortunately, I don't have a crystal ball."

While this may not be what they (or you) want to hear, I can confidently say that my financial advice is based on a track record of providing solutions that give peace of mind to my clients. As I do with them, I'll help you make wise decisions based on what I've learned successfully guiding my clients during the "making work optional" stage of their lives.

CHAPTER 2

WHAT TYPE OF RETIREMENT DO YOU WANT?

And if you don't know where you're going
Any road will take you there!
– *George Harrison*

IN ORDER TO LIVE to the fullest, right up to the end, let's consider a few options, all of which are ways to live out your retirement and spend your resources in a manner that works for you.

THE THELMA AND LOUISE PLAN

At the end of the famous film *Thelma & Louise* (it won the Oscar for Best Original Screenplay in 1991) starring Susan Sarandon and Geena Davis, the two actors must make a decision: (A) Turn themselves into law enforcement for the illegal acts they've committed throughout the film or (B) stomp on the gas of their 1966 Thunderbird convertible and drive off the cliff that's in front of them. The two stars choose option B, which also happens to come pretty close to how some people approach retirement: Spend it all and drive off a cliff when the money runs out.

While I don't recommend the Thelma and Louise Plan, it may be the unintentional consequence for some if they have not planned their retirement properly. Even if the Thelma and Louise Plan feels right for you, I highly suggest reading on, so you gain a clear understanding of what to expect in your retirement journey. As a result, maybe you'll avoid having to drive off that cliff!

THE FIRST-CLASS PLAN

This plan follows the mindset, "If I don't go first class, then my kids will." It doesn't necessarily mean first-class travel all the time, but it does imply you'll be traveling and staying at high-end resorts, dining at fine restaurants, driving a nice car, living in a beautiful home, or buying a second home. With this retirement strategy, you're more focused on enjoying a somewhat indulgent lifestyle because you have the resources or are less focused on leaving a big inheritance behind. The First-Class Plan isn't about refusing to help your children or grandchildren. But it does mean your priority is to take pleasure in retirement while you're healthy and able to do things that are important to you. You seek to enjoy life for as long as you're able.

Perhaps your children and grandchildren are financially self-sufficient. Or maybe you've declared, "I'm the one that earned it, so I'll be the one to spend it!" Whatever is left over when you're gone, your children will inherit, and you'll leave Earth feeling like you've lived your retirement years to the fullest. If you do not have children or relatives to pass your estate to, then maybe you'll decide to be the toast of the town by becoming a contributor or benefactor to charitable organizations. Or maybe you'll plan to have just enough left over in the end so the check to the undertaker won't bounce.

THE FRUGAL PLAN

You've probably heard stories of ordinary people leading modest lives. Upon their deaths, family members find out that Uncle Bill (a barber) or Aunt Sue (a schoolteacher) had accumulated and stashed away an impressive estate that bore little resemblance to his or her humble lifestyle. People like this—call them millionaires next door—epitomize living by the Frugal Plan.

If this describes you, this means you've saved and been building up a nest egg for your retirement years. It's part of your DNA to be a thrifty spender, so now that you're retired, you have no desire to suddenly change course and become a spendthrift. This means you'll continue living in the same manner you always have: looking for bargains, clipping coupons, and refusing to buy things you think are unnecessary.

According to the rules of the Frugal Plan, you may pass down the accumulated assets to the next generation or to charities that reflect causes you care about. Your main objective is to be sure you have enough to maintain your own financial independence and take care of yourself when you reach an age where you require more care or need to move into a retirement community or an assisted care facility. People following the Frugal Plan have become financially successful in their own lives by simply sticking to one of the golden rules about money: Save first and spend less than you earn. Or put another way: Always live within your means.

LEGACY RETIREMENT PLAN

According to this approach, you have enough to continue living your lifestyle while maintaining your goals. These may include financially supporting your children and grandchildren during your retirement, leaving a substantial estate to your kids, and instilling in them your core principles and beliefs. Personally, I like the Legacy Retirement Plan because it allows me to give with a "warm hand" rather than just a stiff "cold one." In other words, gifting to my children and grandchildren while I'm alive allows me to experience the joy and satisfaction of improving their lives.

You may help pay for your kids to get started in their careers or contribute to the down payment of their first home. You may decide to cover all or part of your grandchildren's college tuition.

If you have a large estate and are able to live the lifestyle you most enjoy and help the next generations, as well as make charitable gifting part of your overall financial planning, you most likely will require comprehensive financial and estate planning. The overall goal is to disinherit Uncle Sam and to benefit individuals and organizations most important to you.

At the same time, you may be concerned that your generosity will create "trust fund" babies, which are children that lack the drive you had building your wealth. Trust fund babies don't worry about earning money, and as a result, they may become complacent. They tend to underwork, waiting for the time when they will have an inheritance that will provide for all their needs.

An estate attorney can provide options to address your concerns. One possibility is to set up an "incentive trust" for your children or grandchildren or both. This rewards positive behavior such as establishing careers in specific areas, helping those in need, participating in charitable organizations, or a combination of the preceding. In this way, their focus can be on doing well and doing well for others less fortunate.

You often read about the extremely wealthy such as Bill Gates and Warren Buffet. In the case of these two philanthropists, they have created foundations that help many organizations and have committed to gift 95 percent of their estates to charity upon their deaths. In fact, charitable organizations are frequently funded through the generosity of wealthy families. Many high net-worth families also make charitable work one of their objectives, and a solid estate plan provides many ways to accomplish these goals effectively.

SPECIAL NEEDS RETIREMENT PLAN

Perhaps you have a child or grandchild who has a physical or mental impairment that will always require financial assistance. In this case, you may benefit from a retirement plan that includes a Special Needs Trust (SNT) or setting up a plan that provides ongoing care for a dependent person. An SNT is a trust that provides assistance to the disabled individual without disqualifying him or her from government entitlement benefits such as SSI, Social Security disability benefits, Medicare, or Medicaid benefits. The monies held in an SNT supplement government benefit plan are not considered an asset of the disabled person.

A Special Needs Retirement Plan typically includes a distribution plan that will protect the interests of the incapacitated person, preserving assets to provide the needed care, and be critical to accomplishing your own retirement goals. This may include retaining some amount of life insurance to guarantee the funding of the SNT trust upon your death. Always seek professional guidance in order to develop a special needs trust that aligns with your retirement plan.

SPEND FIRST, THINK LATER PLAN

Under this arrangement, you seek to enjoy what you have and spend more freely during your early retirement years. Another way to describe this is the wait-and-see approach. You may not have much to cover health and medical expenses down the road, but you're not too concerned about this. This lack of worry may be a result of a family history of people with short life spans, or your spouse or you are convinced one of you will greatly outlive the other. The Spend First, Think Later Plan is not the same as the Thelma and Louise Plan because your intention is not to spend everything. Rather, you'll spend up to a point. From there, if you're living longer than your expectations, you'll determine steps you'll need to take to maintain your financial independence.

Unfortunately, one unintended consequence of the wait-and-see approach is conflicts between spouses can arise because the spouse that expects to live long may be concerned he or she may not have enough money to cover his or her long-term expenses. Also, this plan almost always results in one or both spouses being forced to make decisions under stressful circumstances. The lack of planning well ahead of a problem creates a crisis that could otherwise have been avoided.

GETTING YOUR FEET WET FIRST
AND THEN JUMPING IN ALL THE WAY PLAN

For many working couples, they may not always retire at the same time, or they may want to have one spouse continue to earn a paycheck for a set amount of time. Or one spouse, shortly after retiring, may really miss working and be eager to return to the office, perhaps in a different setting. In fact, many retirees are performing consulting work from their homes. This continued connection to the business world provides them a sense of purpose. In this way, the Getting Your Feet Wet First and then Jumping in All the Way Plan provides a smooth glide to retirement—you'll reduce your work pace over several years, instead of just ending your working life in an instant, which can be a shock to the system.

I know of a man who had retired with a healthy nest egg and had no financial worries. But he missed the routine of working so became a Wal-Mart greeter. He enjoyed returning to the workplace albeit in an entirely different setting. While this type of employment may not interest you, you may be in a profession that allows you to work at a reduced pace. That way, you'll avoid plunging into retirement without getting your feet wet first.

Boomers today are not entering normal retirement at age sixty-five or even seventy. They feel healthier and want to continue contributing, so they may be taking on another career. Many companies are finding that boomers make excellent employees, and many are working at new jobs taking on new roles. The low unemployment rate is also a factor for companies that are now hiring seasonal employees to fill the gap, and many of those are boomers!

THE BONNIE AND CLYDE PLAN

You've carefully reviewed all your financial matters. You've performed a thorough analysis of your future financial wellness. Then you ask your significant other, "Who will wear the mask, and who will drive the getaway car?"

CHAPTER 3

EVALUATING YOUR RETIREMENT READINESS

REGARDLESS OF YOUR RETIREMENT approach, you want to have a clear understanding of the advantages and disadvantages of each strategy before you flip the retirement switch. Having meaningful discussions with your professional advisers and family can help in making the decision to retire more enjoyable and less stressful.

There's no one-size-fits-all approach. With that said, for those not interested in the Thelma and Louise Plan (and who have no intention of driving off a cliff) or the Bonnie and Clyde Plan, I've identified five distinct planning stages that people experience throughout their retirement:

1. Transitioning

2. Go-Go Years

3. Slow-Go Years

4. No-Go Years

5. The Exit

Here's a key point about these stages: They do not directly correlate with age. While they may align with age, this is not their purpose. Rather, the stages have more to do with addressing a common concern: How do I maintain both financial and physical independence throughout my retirement life?

With each stage come new challenges. To pass from one stage to the next requires adapting to changes in circumstances, such as health and mobility, and making decisions that can forever impact your overall wellness as well as the lives of your children and grandchildren. In the next section, I'll introduce you to the type of retirement plan that aligns with the five stages of retirement. It's called a Real Retirement Plan.

WHAT IS A REAL RETIREMENT PLAN?

If you understood retirement from TV and online ads, you'd think all retirees were eager and had the funds to buy vineyards, travel around the world on a luxury cruise liner, and invest in a promising start-up. The following, however, is the sobering reality:

- According to *Market Watch* (December 23, 2015), approximately 62 percent of Americans have less than one thousand dollars in their savings accounts, and 21 percent don't even have a savings account.

- According to Google Consumer Survey for personal finance website GOBankingRates.com, about half the US population will retire with less than ten thousand dollars in the bank and Social Security to live on.

- The next 40 percent will have some retirement savings and more investments than the group above. But their nest egg may be too small to last the rest of their lives. They'll need to monitor their spending carefully to have enough money throughout their retirement.

- The next 5 percent of the population will do better. But a significant change in circumstances could quickly diminish their financial security, such as a long-term illness or having the stock market take a plunge soon after retirement, leaving them insufficient time to recover from the financial shock.

- Only the top 5 percent of the population can likely weather financial storms, maintain their current lifestyle, and not have to make major adjustments to spending.

Based on these stats, investing in vineyards and buying costly tickets for cruises are out of the question for most retirees. But that doesn't mean 95 percent of the population (or those comprising the first three groups of retirees in the Google survey) should give up and go for the Thelma and Louise Plan. In fact, regardless of whether you're the top 5 percent of the population, you'll benefit from investing time in real retirement planning, which involves taking an in-depth look into your particular circumstances.

Many companies and government agencies offer consulting or coaching services to those who are entering retirement. These are typically arranged via your employer's HR department.

Unfortunately, the professionals who are appointed to dish out advice often do so in broad strokes in an attempt to apply their recommendations to as many people as possible. They may say, "Don't buy a new home if you're moving to a new area; instead, rent for the first year," or "Try not to make major changes until you have settled into your retirement." This is not real retirement planning.

The primary premise of a Real Retirement Plan is there is no cookie-cutter formula; no simple advice applies to everyone. In order to make decisions that address your individual needs, you must have a true understanding of not just your financial wellness but also your emotional and physical wellbeing.

You need to identify issues you'll face in retirement and address potential problems and pitfalls before they arise.

A Real Retirement Plan is rooted in a balanced approach. Developing one takes more time and thought than a one-size-fits-all program. But the investment is well worth it. Rather than have a generic plan that caters to no one in particular, you'll have a road map that reflects your life—it will guide you through various challenges, take into account your funds today and projected funds of tomorrow, and consider your desires.

YOUR RETIREMENT CHECKLIST

The following are fourteen major items that form part of a Real Retirement Plan (see the appendix for a full list, as well as more details about each of these items):

1. Financial statements updated within the last year

2. Estate documents updated in the last five years

3. Power of attorney (POA) and medical directives updated within the past five years

4. Disposition of personal items

5. Designation of an executor and successor trustee

6. A list of recurring monthly bills

7. Insurance policy information including beneficiaries

8. Account websites and passwords recorded in one safe and easily accessible place

9. Contact information for professional advisers including attorneys, insurance agents, financial planners, accountants, and physicians

10. Annual credit report

11. For business owners, a succession plan

12. Funeral arrangements

13. An articulated vision, discussed with your significant other, of what your hopes and aspirations are in retirement

14. In instances where this is applicable, family meetings regarding your retirement plans

If you have not taken care of all fourteen items, then it's time to focus on pouring a strong retirement foundation, one on which you'll build your Real Retirement Plan that will take you through the five retirement stages. It's also time to take control and decide how you wish to enjoy the second half of the game of life. In part 2, I'll guide you through your foundation's key components, which came about from a client survey I conducted.

PART TWO
Top 5 Retirement Concerns

It's Monday morning. You're in bed and glance at the clock. The digital display reads 8:00 a.m., which is exactly when you're supposed to be at the office. You forgot to set the alarm, and now you're officially late for work. You hop out of bed, leap in the shower, and get dressed as fast as you can. You run to the kitchen and grab a bite of whatever as you head for the door.

"What are you doing?" your significant other yells from the bedroom.

"I'm late for work!" you reply.

"Honey, have you forgotten already?"

You think about the question, and then it hits you. You're not late for anything because this is your first day of retirement.

• • •

In order to write this book, I asked my clients, family, and friends to complete a comprehensive questionnaire I created that focused on issues related to transitioning into retirement and the years that followed. The results provided insights into retirement concerns that most of us have.

When asked, "How do you define retirement and what does it mean to you?" some said they just wanted to get out of the "rat race" of work. Meanwhile, many also said they wanted to continue working in some other capacity for an undefined period. Another way to describe this is "meaningful work," or work that gave them a sense of accomplishment. Then there were other respondents that planned to work until "no longer productive or an asset to their company." Out of these responses, are there any that you relate to?

After reviewing the survey results, I identified the top five concerns respondents provided about retirement. They are as follows:

1. Maintaining health and healthcare options
2. Expectations and financial wellness
3. Aging
4. Social Security and retirement plans
5. Estate planning (legacy)

If you're interested in developing a Real Retirement Plan, then most, if not all, of these concerns are relevant to you as well.

In the following five chapters, after introducing each issue, I'll provide possible solutions to build a strong retirement foundation.

CHAPTER 4

MAINTAINING HEALTH AND HEALTHCARE OPTIONS

"**I WISH I HAD** a better understanding of Medicare and Social Security." This was the feedback one survey respondent provided. Has this concern crossed your mind as well? No doubt, healthcare for those retiring before reaching age sixty-five can be more difficult than ever because the choices have changed dramatically over the past few years.

If you were employed with a company that had a medical plan, two common healthcare options during your transition phase are Consolidated Omnibus Budget Reconciliation Act (COBRA) and Health Savings Account (HAS).

You may be eligible for COBRA from your employer. This program allows you to remain enrolled under your current healthcare plan for up to eighteen months, but not after you've passed age sixty-five.

Another option for those under age sixty-five and not enrolled in Medicare is to establish a Health Savings Account. This is a tax-favored plan designed to pay for qualified medical expenses for the individual or family. You establish an HSA by making tax-deductible contributions that can be invested and used to pay for certain medical expenses. A qualifying high-deductible health insurance plan must be obtained to partner with the HSA.

The monies in the HSA accumulate without incurring income taxes, and the distributions to pay for medical services are not taxable income. The person who opened an HSA owns it, and it is portable. Note that there are limits to the annual amounts that can be contributed for an individual or family.

If you were self-employed, you may want to continue your current plan if the business is still operating during your retirement transition. But if you had employees and were covered under a small group plan, you may need to think about obtaining an individual health insurance plan because the group plan may no longer be available to you individually once the business is closed.

DO I NEED TO MAINTAIN LIFE INSURANCE?

The simple answer is "it depends." You first need to think of why you initially applied for your policy. In most cases, life insurance is purchased to create cash for the survivors to provide them income and financial resources that you did not have an opportunity to accumulate before your untimely passing. Once you retire, however, you have presumably accumulated the necessary resources to provide for yourself and spouse. So, from that viewpoint, there may be little need for life insurance after retirement.

But let's imagine your husband or wife suffers a long-term illness or becomes incapacitated. After he or she passes and all your spouse's bills are paid, how much savings will you have to support you for the rest of your life?

If that is a concern, as a first step, consider purchasing long-term care (LTC) insurance. Next, think about having some form of permanent life insurance. This is cash-value life insurance, which is different from term insurance. Term life insurance usually terminates before you do. In fact, less than 2 percent of term policies pay a benefit. Unfortunately, buying permanent life insurance during your retirement transition phase is not only very expensive, but it is also more difficult to obtain than if you were younger because your health may disqualify you for the best rates. For this reason, I've recommended to my clients they purchase permanent life insurance when they're younger, usually under age sixty, in order to provide for survivors in the future. Another reason to buy permanent life insurance is to provide a guaranteed benefit amount to your children—in other words, insurance in this instance provides a financial legacy. Or permanent life insurance can benefit a special needs child or a charity.

Another option for those who do not need the income from their individual retirement accounts (IRAs) and only take out the required amount each year (I'll discuss required withdrawals in chapter 7) is to use the distributions to pay for a life insurance policy that creates a tax-free benefit to surviving family members or to a charity.

As far as estate tax laws are concerned, with the changes in the laws, the need for life insurance to help pay for the estate tax liability now affects only a very small percentage of the population.

In the end, buying life insurance may come down to a personal choice. In my experience, I've observed that my clients' life insurance beneficiaries are usually very appreciative of having some tax-free monies to provide for their own future financial needs.

THE AFFORDABLE CARE ACT (ACA)

Many different healthcare plans on the market fall under the ACA, which is also known as Obamacare. At the time of this book's publication, the likelihood Obamacare will remain intact is low, which means legislators will most likely replace or dramatically modify it.

ACA or not, in general, your options really boil down to only a few: the government-based plans, employer plans that have retiree healthcare benefits, and independent insurance company plans that meet the requirements of the ACA.

Unfortunately, most of these plans become unaffordable because premiums have been rising by double-digit amounts annually with no end in sight. Therefore, they may not provide the intended benefits. Having a good affordable health insurance plan in place before retirement is a critical issue that needs to be fully addressed, especially if retiring prior to being eligible for Medicare, which is age sixty-five.

Plans are available that can provide the needed coverage; however, it is up to you to seek professional guidance on this matter to obtain the plan best suited for you and your family.

MEDICARE OVERVIEW

In my small research study, several respondents wished they had a better understanding of Medicare as they approached age sixty-five.

It is very important to understand exactly what Medicare benefits are, so you can be prepared to pay the deductible and any co-payments, plus the uncovered services. Because Medicare rules are constantly changing, especially the drug benefits in Part D, it is important to review your Medicare choices each year during the open enrollment period, which is typically between October 15 and December 7. This should be done in conjunction with a review of your supplemental health coverage, either from prior employer health plans or Medigap insurance plans.

There are a number of issues that can impact your decisions as to which Medicare plan is best for you. Here are a few to think about:

- Will you still be working when you turn age sixty-five?

- Will your employer health plan continue to provide coverage throughout your retirement?

- Is your employer health plan a "creditable" health plan, meaning, does it pay at least as much as the Medicare Part D? If not, you may be in for a surprise when signing up for Part D and incur a penalty.

- Do you plan to travel or live part of the year in another location, such as spending winters in Florida? If this is the case, traditional Medicare may be better than enrolling in Medicare Advantage plans because you will have greater access to providers wherever you are located.

- Did you participate in a Health Savings Account? Once you enroll in Medicare Part A, you can no longer contribute to an HSA.

- You could incur penalties for delaying enrollment into Part B or Part D. The penalties are based on how many months of delay, and the penalty is applied to all future Medicare premiums, for life!

- Have you reviewed your Medigap policy each year to determine what is covered and what amounts you may still be liable for paying?

- Medicare and Medicaid do not provide long-term care benefits.

MEDICARE'S MULTIPLE PERSONALITIES

Medicare has four parts: A, B, C, and D. These are all considered a "fee for service" system, and the participant can choose to go to any doctor or health facility that accepts Medicare payments. Note that Medicare typically does not provide dental, vision, or hearing benefits or has only minimal benefits at best, unless you choose the Medicare Advantage Plan. Thus, after age sixty-five, you may need to obtain individual dental and vision coverage.

Let's look at each to see what amounts you may need to pay out of pocket. Note that the premiums shown are for 2018, and they will increase each year by a cost of living adjustment (COLA) determined by the government.

Medicare Part A

At age sixty-five, you may be required to enroll into Medicare Part A, which is hospital insurance. There is no cost for Part A; however, some employer group plans may require you to participate in Part B, which is medical insurance that carries a premium (Part B is discussed in the next section). If you are continuing to work for an employer with more than twenty employees and you have a qualified, high deductible plan with an HSA or HSA-R, then you may be able to defer enrollment in Part A. In those cases, it can be more beneficial to defer, as you will be able to continue contributing to the HSA plan. Once you enroll in Medicare Part A or enroll in Social Security, the HSA contributions must cease. The decision comes down to determining the cost differential between continuing in a qualified HSA plan or enrollment into Medicare. Consideration should be given to not just premium but also what your medical needs may be going forward. The healthier you are the more beneficial retaining the HSA will be. If you plan to work until age seventy, then continuing the HAS may be best choice, as you will be able to continue building up savings in the HSA plan that can be used upon retirement.

Part A will cover the first sixty days of a hospital stay (all but $1,340 of co-payments and deductible), and from the sixty-first day to the ninetieth day, you'll pay $335 per day. From the ninety-first day, the coinsurance amount is $670 per day for each lifetime reserve day up to sixty days over your lifetime. Beyond that, you are responsible for all costs. If you need post-hospital skilled nursing care in a care facility or rehab center, Medicare covers the first twenty days, but you are on the hook for $165 per day thereafter. The maximum time Medicare will cover is one hundred days. Afterwards, you are on your own to pay for the hospital care if you do not have a supplemental Medigap policy.

Medicare Part B

This covers all medical expenses for doctor's services, both inpatient and outpatient. There is an annual deductible, which is currently $183.

From there, Medicare pays 80 percent of the approved amount for most doctor services. You are responsible to pay the balance. Note that mental health services are only covered at 50 percent.

The cost for Part B starts at $134 per month but increases depending upon your actual reported income on your tax return. The current maximum cost is $428.60 per month. If you have higher earnings or generate large capital gains from the sale of property or investments, this monthly amount can become a significant issue because the Medicare premiums will be affected for the following two years! If you enroll in Part B before you start receiving Social Security retirement benefits, you will then receive a quarterly bill from Medicare to pay the premiums. Once you start receiving Social Security, your premiums will automatically be deducted from your monthly Social Security payment.

MONEY SAVING TIP: *Keep in mind that when you first retire, your prior year income may be much higher than in your first year of retirement, which could cause the premium to be at a higher level. You need to submit a request to the Social Security Administration once you have retired to obtain an exception so that the premiums will reflect your retirement income. Doing so can save you hundreds of dollars a month! You should go to the Social Security office and file the form to make the adjustment once you have retired.*

Medicare Part C

Medicare Part C, or Medicare Advantage, combines Medicare Parts A and B into one plan, as well as makes available some other benefits. Under Part C, you have several options: health maintenance organizations (HMOs), point of service (POS), preferred provider organizations (PPOs), provider sponsored organizations (PSOs), and private fee for service plans. Some of the plans may offer dental and vision coverage as well. Medicare C is priced based upon the alternative you choose, but note that having Part C means you do not need a Medigap insurance policy, which I'll describe in this chapter. In addition, choices will depend upon where you live.

Medicare Part D

You may also need to enroll in Part D, which is prescription drug coverage. The cost for medications will be dependent upon the actual drug prescribed and if it is a generic or brand name. If you're taking prescription medications, you can visit the government website and find out if the medication is covered or how much it will cost you if it's not. This may help in making the decision between choosing Medicare A, B, or D or if you should enroll in Medicare Advantage. Note that you can also make this decision annually during the open enrollment period each fall.

Medicare Supplement Policies (Medigap)

These policies are sold by independent insurance companies and provide benefits to supplement the amounts payable under Medicare, including copayments, deductibles, and coinsurance. The government has standardized the various plans to provide consumer protection and to reduce the misunderstandings about what coverage is available. As a result, the only difference between the plans from insurance companies is the cost and the company ratings.

In regard to ratings, I recommend you check your state insurance website for ratings of insurance companies licensed in your state. Medigap policies are guaranteed issue if acquired within six months of turning age sixty-five.

• • •

In the next chapter, "Expectations and Financial Wellness," we'll explore the second concern.

CHAPTER 5

EXPECTATIONS AND FINANCIAL WELLNESS

NUMBER TWO AMONG THE top-five concerns respondents had about retirement was expectations. Specifically, expectations refer to understanding how you see your retirement years from both a personal and financial perspective. By addressing your expectations, you'll have a clear picture of what you can reasonably spend in order to maintain your financial independence throughout your retirement life.

Here are a few observations respondents had in regard to expectations as they related to the transition into retirement:

- Not having a paycheck and worrying about spending.

- The impact of new routines, not having your calendar filled, establishing new contacts, or having too few emails can be unsettling!

- The finality of my career and filling the void is crucial to having a smooth transition.

- Reconnecting with my spouse now that we are together 24-7 can be a challenge!

Can you relate to any of these concerns? Regarding the last point, retirement can cause conflict between you and your significant other. Many couples are unpleasantly surprised when retirement rolls around. They find themselves suddenly disagreeing over matters that had not created conflict before.

Meanwhile, conventional wisdom tells us retirement is a period of our lives that is carefree and relaxing. But for many, it's just the opposite. It can be anxiety inducing and stressful. Just thinking about moving or downsizing can cause a great deal of worry. In fact, the transition into retirement can be one of the most emotionally taxing periods in your lifetime. You may feel trapped under the pressure to decide where you'll live, possibly leaving your familiar and comfortable environment and someday moving to a place where you'll be surrounded by "old" people.

In order to make your transition period as successful as possible, you need to have a solid understanding of what retirement will look like for you and your spouse or partner. And you want to be sure you have these conversations during the retirement transition phase. Enlisting a mental health professional to help you navigate this transition period may improve how you communicate with your spouse and express, as well as deal with, the various emotions you're experiencing during your transition.

THE RETIREMENT EXPECTATIONS EXERCISE

One easy step to avoid disappointment is to complete a simple but effective exercise I developed. All you need is a pen and paper. Answer the following questions. (These also appear in appendix D.) And if you have a significant other, have that person also create his or her own responses:

- What are your vision and your personal expectations in retirement?

- What is on your bucket list?

- What are your biggest concerns for this period of your life?

- What activities have you talked about doing but never found the time to do before while working?

- Have you thought about relocating? If so, where?

- How comfortable are you managing your finances?

- If you were lying on your deathbed, what would you regret not having done?

- Can you identify what is most important to you at this stage of your life?

- What is the plan for the ultimate disposition of your assets?

- Will having grandchildren influence any of the preceding answers?

- If you are partnered, are you each aligned with the expectations, goals, and wishes of the other?

Once you've answered your questions individually, share them with each other and compare. Did you both have the same expectations about retirement? Identify and discuss where you have common interests and ones that aren't aligned. By both of you expressing your feelings, you'll be able to make decisions together going forward that reflect both of your perspectives.

DISCLAIMER: *Not being totally aligned is normal. Think of it as an opportunity to learn more about each other, resolve possible conflicts before they arise, improve the skill of compromise, and find alternatives that will make both of you happy.*

Keep in mind that your relationship in retirement will not be the same as it was while one or both were working. Anticipating this change ahead of time will avoid conflict in the future.

When your perspectives are different, and you can't come to a mutual understanding, working with a mental health professional may provide the objectivity you need in order to make decisions that benefit your lives as a couple.

LOSS OF A PAYCHECK

One major disruptive force that can instantly lower your retirement expectations and hamper your financial wellness is a loss of a paycheck. In my survey, one respondent described being unexpectedly laid off from his job.

One day Richard had a bright future, and in an instant, his whole world dropped out from beneath him. Prior to receiving the bad news, Richard's schedule was always full and managed by his assistant. Now that he was out of work, he sat in his home office staring at a computer screen. But at fifty-five years old, Richard didn't have the luxury to stay unemployed because he needed income to support his family.

At the same time, Richard was stuck in a frozen state of disbelief for several days, and it took weeks before he was able to even think about looking for a new job. Thankfully, he found work and retired twelve years later. The experience of being let go at fifty-five years old taught him lessons that he carried with him in his retirement. Richard realized his life could dramatically change at any moment, and he no longer took his financial security and stability for granted.

Richard's difficult experience illustrates a point that all of us must keep in mind: The time when you retire can sometimes be out of your control. You may have been let go as result of a company merger or downsizing. You or a family member may have a health issue that results in you having to retire prematurely. The closer you are to your retirement age, the sharper the sting of a sudden lay off or health scare because it can derail any retirement plans you had developed prior to receiving the bad news.

The impact of an early or partial retirement can be devastating if you haven't been saving and investing. Given the unpredictable times we're living in today, I recommend always hoping for the best and preparing for the worst. In other words, do not assume the job you have today will carry you through to retirement or your present state of health will be the same when you reach retirement.

So, what is one way to prepare for the worst? Take charge of your retirement planning without delay.

Over the years, I've listened to many reasons why my clients chose to delay investing in their retirement. One frequent reason I've heard goes something like, "I'll wait till my kids graduate from college before maximizing my retirement contributions."

Unfortunately, postponing investing in retirement will cost you over the long term. Waiting too long can make the difference between having enough money to support your retirement lifestyle and having to drastically decrease your standard of living.

For many, current expenses make it nearly impossible to save. No doubt, investing in retirement can feel like a heavy burden. Even saving 1 percent, as I once saw pitched in a retirement advertisement, may seem implausible. For many, doing so would require making a change to lifestyle in their working years. But better to make some changes early (no matter how small), rather than waking up needing more resources but without options.

RETIREMENT TRANSITION TIP: *Sudden changes in your schedule can be stressful. In order to make your retirement transition period as smooth as possible, I recommend creating routines that mimic certain aspects of life prior to retirement.*

If you worked for a company, one disruptive force is the weekly, bimonthly, or monthly paycheck you'll stop receiving. In order to avoid the shock to the system of no longer receiving a paycheck, you can easily maintain a paycheck-like pattern by duplicating the timing of the income you receive during your retirement. But rather than the funds coming from your employer, they'd arrive from your nest egg. Whether the monies are coming from personal investment accounts or IRAs, they can be directly deposited to your bank account on any specified day of the month—just as they had been while you were working.

Consider having the same or around the same amount you received from your paycheck deposited into your bank account. If you're receiving a pension or Social Security, you'll typically receive these payments at the beginning of the month, so consider having your deposit from the investment portfolio fall in the middle of the month. That way, you'll be receiving checks at least twice per month.

I've found this simple strategy helps with maintaining your financial routine. It allows you to continue the same monthly bill-pay habits you've always had. In addition, this is a major consideration for many who have lived on a budget or had to clip coupons to make ends meet because it ensures funds are available when they're needed. For others, this tip maintains peace of mind that comes from receiving a paycheck every two weeks. My recommendations to maintain your financial routine is the perfect segue to the third concern among the top five my survey respondents had: aging.

CHAPTER 6
AGING

I always knew I'd get old.

But how fast it happened was a bit of a surprise!

– *Unknown*

NUMBER THREE AMONG THE top-five concerns respondents had about retirement was aging. One respondent commented, "It hurts to be alive and aging as a woman."

Given that pithy comment, let's start with women and aging first. It's well known that women generally outlive men. Because many women will be charged with managing their financial lives long after their husbands have died, it is important that they have a full understanding of their finances early in their marriage and in retirement—not just when they've lost their spouses due to death or divorce. The harsh reality at this point is that being tasked to make major financial decisions may quickly overwhelm a person who has never had to manage finances in the past.

If you're married or partnered and uncertain whether you've been out of the financial loop, answer the following questions:

- Do you know what your financial statements show?

- Do you know where all your financial accounts are located?

- Do you have a list of the accounts and any associated passwords?

If you answered no to any of the questions, it's time to grab the reins of your financial life. One simple way to gain control of your finances is to take responsibility for paying the bills if you've deferred this task to your significant other.

RETIREMENT TRANSITION TIP: *Have you joined AARP yet? Although the organization's claim to fame is social welfare and advocacy for retirees and elders, the thirty-eight-million-member strong nonprofit has become a major insurance and investment organization. If you can dodge some of its aggressive sales tactics, you'll find AARP is a solid resource for people nearing retirement or already in retirement. Information can be found on www.aarp. org. It also has dental, vision, and hearing plans for members.*

AGING AND CHANGING ROUTINES

One of the biggest challenges I've witnessed my clients experience in the transition phase is developing new routines. As humans, we are creatures of habit. For proof, look at how infants and children thrive when we set up routines such as bath time, meals, reading time, naptime, school, and bedtime.

Whether we loved our jobs or dreaded showing up to the office every day, our work lives took up a significant amount of time and gave us a daily routine. With retirement around the corner, we will soon be responsible for our schedules. From deciding what time we'll wake up in the morning to how we'll fill our waking hours, we're in charge. While on the surface, this may sound exactly like what we wanted, unless we've invested time considering our schedules, we may find ourselves feeling uneasy with the sudden flexibility.

In fact, it can take a bit of time just to determine when to get out of bed! And once we finally do decide what time to wake up, we may find ourselves asking, "What am I going to eat for breakfast?" and "When is my golf tee time?"

Asking yourself basic questions like these is completely normal. After all, you've had a certain working routine for most of your life, and now it is gone. So now that you're retired, what will take its place?

To avoid the stress associated with changing routines in retirement, refer to the Retirement Expectations Exercise in appendix D. Answering these sometimes-uncomfortable transition questions before you retire will help you adjust to new routines that will come about in your retirement. As with most major changes in life, sorting out what is really important to you and what is trivial and doing it well will take time. And the older we are, the more our patterns have been established and the more time and energy we'll need to develop new habits.

I encourage you to look at retirement as a new opportunity to do some of the things you always talked about doing but never found the time while working. Retirement should be celebrated, so consider taking a trip shortly after retirement—whether you're single or have a spouse. This could be the dream trip you had put off taking. If you're married, think of this as your second (or first) honeymoon. A trip is a positive, fun, and memorable way to mark your transition into retired life and to signal you're embarking on a new and exciting adventure.

RETIREMENT TRANSITION TIP: *As a successful professional, your smartphone calendar and address book were filled with meetings, appointments, and contacts. So now that you're transitioning into retirement, you may find it disappointing to see a blank calendar that was once packed with events. A simple way to avoid the letdown of a smartphone stripped of information is to set up your calendar and contact list under your new role as a transitioning retiree.*

On your smartphone, start by keeping business contacts allowed by your employer, and then stay in touch with your colleagues. Also, from doctor's appointments to meeting friends for golf, make it a habit to put events in your phone's calendar. Leveraging your smartphone is a simple way to maintain a routine that you had relied on every day prior to transition into retirement.

AGING AND DATING

One survey respondent said the following:

**Being single and dating post retirement
is a very different experience for men and women.**

From my experience working with widows and widowers, I've observed that men in their sixties and seventies tend to date more often than their female counterparts. I've asked my widowed clients about this. A common reply I've received is they think men in those age ranges often seek out women twenty years younger than themselves. For many men, this is a defense mechanism; they're seeking someone to care for them as they get older. Other men are in denial about their own aging!

Hollywood has also brought this topic to the forefront. If you haven't seen the 2003 film *Something's Gotta Give,* starring Jack Nicholson and Diane Keaton, I highly recommend it. Jack Nicholson's character is dating the stunning young-adult daughter of Diane Keaton's character. The movie has a series of fun twists and describes the dilemma my female clients have described to me—they often feel as though they are destined to live their lives without another partner. But this certainly doesn't have to be the case.

AGING FOR MEN AND WOMEN

Have you experienced a knee or hip replacement? What about cataracts? Have you had an organ transplant? We are becoming a generation of body-part replacements! Continued medical advancements may offer an opportunity to significantly extend our lives. The key concern is not living longer but rather being able to enjoy living longer.

The moment we're born, the aging process starts. But it accelerates as we enter the retirement stage of our lives. If you've had to take care of aging parents, then you know all too well how difficult it is when it's up to you to make their life decisions. Although the experience of caring for aging parents is never easy, it has given you valuable insight about retirement you otherwise wouldn't have.

If your goal is to maintain your personal independence, then you must address your long-term healthcare earlier than later, so you don't leave difficult decisions about your life for someone else to make on your behalf.

The more you plan your retirement stages ahead of time, the more secure you'll be. You'll also have greater peace of mind and not place the burden of major decisions about your life on your children, other family members, or even strangers.

I recommend having an open and honest conversation about what is really important to you, and what you want to have happen when you're no longer able to care for yourself. This may be done through a family meeting or meeting with a trusted friend. Each family is different. Thus, what you'll discuss during your particular meeting will vary based on your family dynamic.

Possible topics of conversation include the following:

- Your retirement plans.

- Who will be responsible for carrying out your intentions.

- What your intentions are concerning your living circumstances and care in the event you become incapacitated.

- Deciding who will be the executor, successor trustee, or attorney-in-fact before you list them in your wills, trusts, powers of attorney, and medical directives. Keep in mind, the roles you are asking them to take can be difficult, and you want to be sure they agree to take on that responsibility.

The alternative to having a family member or friend take charge is to have a professional such as a law firm, bank trust department, or independent trust company act on your behalf.

In addition, you should consider appointing someone to oversee bill paying and maintaining the financial records. In certain cases, enrolling the help of an elder law attorney may be the most beneficial in making sure that you receive the help you need and that your estate is in solid shape in order to maximize benefits to you and your beneficiaries.

In my own situation, after my dad passed away, my three sisters and I met with my mom to receive her input about her plans for the future without my father around. We asked her what she wanted to do as far as her living situation and with all of the family belongings in the house.

During our family meeting, we grown-up children proposed having our mother move closer to one of us. But she had a different plan. First, she wanted to remain in her current house for the short term and decide later if she would move.

The closest sibling lived four hours away from her, so her decision to stay put caused us all to worry about her wellbeing. She convinced us she would be fine, and we went along with her wishes. In regard to the household belongings, we developed a plan to distribute her possessions upon her passing.

One of Mom's best ideas was to color code her belongings. She had one of four colors correspond with each of us, and she placed different colored stickers on the back of items such as furniture indicating who would receive what item.

After Mom passed, we had a treasure hunt in the family home identifying the items she passed to each of us. If we wanted to trade items, we negotiated amongst ourselves.

Our mother's plan was to divide her estate effectively and avoid sibling conflict afterwards. It was successful on both fronts. After she passed, we settled her estate in a timely manner.

I think aging in retirement is one of the most challenging times in your life. One day everything seems fine, and the next day you can be in a doctor's office or hospital receiving difficult news that will impact the rest of your life. Fortunately, overcoming difficult times is much easier when you have a team working on your behalf to help you deal with whatever comes your way. Having a Real Retirement Plan and a professional team, which may include a lawyer, financial adviser, banker, CPA, insurance agent, mental health professional, and doctor, is imperative to help guide you and your family. A solid team will allow you to make the most of your retirement years. For example, do you have a family physician? Do you regularly meet with him or her for check-ups? When you are at home and ill, have you designated a person who will monitor your medications? Planning ahead can greatly extend your life and the quality of your life in retirement.

AGING IN THE RIGHT PLACE

One respondent shared the following:

> I built my home several years ago with the plan to remain in it for as long as possible. That's why I installed wider doors, designed it so I had the ability to live on one floor, had a second bedroom built as a handicap bedroom, and added a handicap bathroom on the first floor and a handicap accessible entrance and exit from the house. I plan to stay here to the end if possible!

Aging in place is a term that describes people in retirement living out their lives in their own home. The most common reason people seek to age in place is they want to remain in their own environment and maintain their independence and social connections—rather than be admitted into a care facility. The difficulty with aging in place is your ability to maintain a home becomes more challenging and expensive because you may need to hire people to perform the upkeep you previously managed to do yourself in the past.

Aging in place does not necessarily mean staying in the family home forever. Instead, it may involve downsizing into a smaller residence, moving into an adult retirement community, moving closer to children and grandchildren, or any combination of the preceding. In most cities today, you have multiple living options that didn't exist even a generation ago. From first floor master bedrooms and adult (over age fifty-five) communities to continuing care retirement communities (CCRCs), retired people have an unprecedented number of choices today. We will discuss these more thoroughly in the Slow-Go and No-Go Years in chapters 11 and 12, respectively.

For now, it's important to consider moving into a retirement community sooner rather than later. Doing so sooner will give you the time necessary to form new relationships, and it will provide a longer period of freedom from the headaches associated with maintaining a home. Most of these communities designed for retired people provide full maintenance of the exterior of the homes and grounds. In addition, my clients tell me they are more comfortable taking long trips. They can lock and leave for extended periods without worry because they know their homes are being looked after.

LONG TERM CARE (LTC) INSURANCE

According to the Centers for Disease Control and Prevention, in 2012 approximately 58,500 paid, regulated long-term care providers were in the United States. That number included adult day centers, home health agencies, hospice, nursing homes, and residential care communities.

Among those seeking long-term care providers, especially assisted living, most are women. In fact, according to the Assisted Living Federation of America (ALFA), assisted living communities have a seven to one ratio of women to men.

As you read previously in this book, the reason more women than men live in assisted living is simply that women tend to outlive men. In general, men live about seven years less than their female counterparts. With that said, the average lifespan for men in the United States is increasing. According to the Social Security Administration (SSA), a man reaching age 65 today can expect to live until age 84.3, on average, while a 65-year-old woman can expect to live until age 86.6. With men living longer than ever before, it stands to reason that men will be entering assisted living communities in higher numbers in the coming years.

Today's assisted living resident has the following profile:

- She is a mobile female around eighty-seven years old.

- While she is mostly independent, she does require some help with at least two or three daily living activities such as bathing, dressing, eating, and medication management.

- She may also have chronic conditions such as osteoporosis or high blood pressure.

For women and men, the cost of care is increasing rapidly. In fact, the cost can start at a few thousand dollars per month to live in an assisted care facility. From there, the amount can skyrocket to over ten thousand dollars per month to live in a memory care facility. Some facilities require a buy-in, while others simply require monthly payments. In most cases, the buy-in will allow individuals to have much lower monthly payments for their care, but they may lose a portion of the monies deposited up front. While many facilities have a refund policy, you are not likely to receive a full refund of the amount you paid to enter the facility.

Then there are "pay as you go" communities. They will generally have higher monthly payments for providing the care. But you do not have to tie up your monies in large up-front deposits. Each has pros and cons, and the choice is dependent upon your own personal financial situation.

The cost of buying an LTC policy has risen in recent years mainly due to the fact that people are actually using the benefits! In fact, after age sixty-five, you have a greater than 70 percent chance of needing some form of assisted care, either at home or in a facility. If you're not married and do not plan to leave an inheritance, then having LTC insurance may not be necessary.

However, if you have a spouse and want to try to preserve assets, then buying an LTC policy can be very beneficial. LTC insurance may not cover all costs, but it can greatly reduce the amount of withdrawals from your accumulated resources in the event you need care. If you require long-term care, LTC insurance will help preserve your assets, leaving your spouse with the resources needed for his or her future care. In most cases, you'll recover the cost of LTC insurance within a year after obtaining benefits.

In order to navigate the complicated LTC waters, I suggest contacting an LTC insurance specialist. This person can help you identify the amount of coverage appropriate for your circumstances. Before you make the call, review the following list that describes the components that should be part of any good LTC coverage. Keep in mind that current policies do not require a hospital stay to qualify as they did twenty years ago. If you have an older policy, be sure to review its terms, definitions, and benefits to be clear about how the insurance company will pay benefits:

When to buy: The cost of LTC insurance is based upon your age and health condition. The longer you wait, the higher the premium and the risk you have in not qualifying for the insurance. I recommend you apply when you are between the ages of fifty-five and sixty-five. The qualification is more about your morbidity, which are chronic issues that may reduce your mobility, versus mortality. However, you can apply for coverage generally up to age eighty.

Qualified policies: These meet certain requirements the federal government has established that allow the premiums to be treated as medical expenses. This means they can qualify, with certain limitations, as a medical expense itemized tax deduction under IRS Schedule A.

Activities of Daily Living (ADLs): These are eating, bathing, toileting, continence, dressing, and transferring (getting in and out of bed or a chair on your own). Your inability to perform these, or a certain number of these, activities determines the need for LTC benefits. In most policies, having two ADLs is required for the policy benefits to be initiated. There are also specific conditions such as dementia, head injuries, AIDS, and old age that can qualify for LTC benefits to be initiated.

Benefit period: This reflects the LTC insurance coverage period, which may span from one year to an entire lifetime. The longer the benefit period, the higher the premium will be. Unless you have a family history of dementia and family members needing care for extended periods, I would consider a policy benefit period between three to five years because that would cover over 95 percent of the risk. Because of their longevity, women may need to have a longer benefit period than men.

Benefit amount: This should be based upon your overall financial situation, your other income sources, and the cost for care in your geographical area. In most cases, having an amount that would cover at least 50 percent of the cost of care in an assisted care facility should be sufficient.

Benefit payment method: In general, you have two methods of basing payments: daily or monthly. Daily benefits pay up to a maximum per day of service provided. If the cost is higher than the maximum, the individual is responsible for the balance. Under a monthly benefit, the amount of daily expense incurred may be fully covered up to the total amount of the monthly limit. I typically recommend this option, especially if you plan to age in place and you don't require care services daily.

Inflation protection: This is the most critical component of LTC insurance and the option that can have the most impact upon your premiums. The younger you are when you buy the insurance, the more important inflation protection becomes.

In recent years, the cost of LTC coverage has increased for both existing and newly issued policies. For existing policyholders, especially those that have had coverage for more than ten years, the cost increase can be offset by reducing the inflation amount. For example, a 5 percent compound inflation benefit may be modified to a 2 or 3 percent compound, or it may retain the 5 percent without compounding, and the premium may be about the same. LTC insurance companies are sending notices of the premium changes. They are informing customers of options such as paying the higher premium or reducing the inflation benefit or the benefit amount or period in order to keep the premium level. If you receive an offer from your insurance company, be sure to review the options with a professional to determine the best choice for your particular circumstances. Generally, if you are over age seventy, a reduction in the inflation factor will keep the premium in line with your current premium.

Deductible (waiting period): The deductible is not a specific dollar amount. Instead, it is a number of days in which care is provided before the benefits begin. Some policies do not have a waiting period, while the waiting period for others may range from thirty days to six months.

In the next chapter, you'll learn about the fourth among the top-five retirement concerns: Social Security and retirement plans.

CHAPTER 7

SOCIAL SECURITY AND RETIREMENT PLANS

NUMBER FOUR AMONG THE top-five concerns respondents had about retirement was Social Security retirement benefits and distribution plans. Let's begin with Social Security.

One respondent commented, "I wish I had a better understanding of how Social Security would impact my cash flow and income taxes."

The Social Security Administration and its associated retirement benefits were enacted back in 1935 as a way to provide a safety net for workers who had no other retirement resources, especially after the 1929 stock market crash.

Who is eligible to receive Social Security benefits? Any person who has earned forty credits is considered fully insured. Forty credits generally mean having been employed for ten years and earning more than $5,200 per year. The worker benefits are based upon the amount of income earned up to the maximum Social Security level known as the "wage base." This wage base is indexed for inflation and places a cap on benefits a person can receive, regardless of earnings. You can obtain a benefits statement directly from the Social Security Administration by visiting www.ssa.gov.

At the time Social Security was introduced, the average life expectancy was sixty-five years. As you're likely well aware, life expectancy for an infant born today is about age seventy-six—oh my, how times have changed! As we age, life expectancy increases as long as we remain healthy. In other words, if you or your spouse is in good health (as in no chronic illness or disease) at age sixty-five, your life expectancy is about twenty-one more years, which means you'll live to age eighty-six on average. When you think about how long you'll need to support yourself between your retirement transition and until you reach eighty-six years old, it may work in your favor to wait until age seventy to start receiving Social Security benefits. However, in certain instances, this may not be the best decision for you. For instance, if you need the income sooner to pay for basic needs or you have poor health, it may be best to start receiving SSA retirement benefits as soon as you are eligible. But if you can wait, the reward will be an increase in the payment you'll receive. It will be equal to about 8 percent per year for each year delayed.

According to SSA, full retirement age (FRA) is the age at which you are eligible for full SS benefits. FRA is not the same for everyone. SSA is phasing in later FRAs for those born after 1954 to take into account the fact we are living longer, and often not retiring at what once was the magic sixty-five years.

For example, if your FRA is age sixty-six (which means you were born in 1954 or earlier) and you defer for four years (that is, you wait till you're seventy years old) you'll increase the monthly amount you receive by a whopping 32 percent.

This is not an investment increase; it is an actuarial increase on the retirement benefit. An actuarial increase means that under a life expectancy table, you will have a shorter period to collect Social Security. If you live to the age of life expectancy, the total amount paid may be the same regardless of when you start. The goal is to outlive your life expectancy to get the most out of the government!

Within your family history, if no one lives past age eighty, or if you are in poor health during the transition phase, you may want to start receiving benefits at FRA or earlier. The breakeven calculation between starting at FRA and deferring until age seventy is living until about age eighty-two. The longer you live past age eighty-two, the more beneficial it will be to have deferred the start of Social Security retirement until age seventy.

If you decide to begin Social Security benefits early, you will receive a reduced benefit that is permanent. Go to the government Social Security website (ssa.gov) to get up-to-date information on how your benefits will be affected by starting earlier than your FRA.

In the next sections, we'll explore various Social Security benefit options you have, depending on your particular circumstances: spousal, children, divorced spouse, and death benefit to a surviving spouse.

Spousal Benefit: If you're married and your spouse has obtained his or her SS benefits, you can also apply for SS benefits as early as age sixty-two at a reduced amount. If you're a widow, benefits can begin as early as age sixty. If both spouses have earned enough credits to obtain benefits, the lower-income spouse may be able to claim benefits based upon his or her own Social Security earnings record or that of the spouse, whichever gives the higher benefit.

Note that once you elect to take early benefits (before FRA), the reduction is permanent. However, if you elected early benefits and your spouse started his or hers at FRA and later dies, you could get the full amount of your spouse's benefit if greater than your current benefit.

Children's Benefit: When a parent dies, children's benefit is payable to dependent children under age eighteen or dependent children disabled before age twenty-two. In the case of deceased husbands or wives, the surviving spouse will also receive the same benefit until the youngest child turns sixteen, or if she or he is disabled before age twenty-two.

Divorced Spouse: If you are divorced, are at least sixty-two, and your marriage lasted for a minimum of ten years and your ex-spouse was a fully insured worker, then you are entitled to receive an amount as a spousal benefit—as long as it is greater than the amount based upon your spouse's earnings record. Keep in mind this benefit is not negotiated in a divorce settlement because it is a government entitlement benefit and not a marital asset. The divorced spouse can also receive a survivor's benefit upon reaching age sixty. Or if disabled, he or she is eligible to receive the benefit earlier.

Death Benefit to a Surviving Spouse: A lump sum of $255 is payable to the surviving spouse for burial expenses. If there is no surviving spouse, no benefit is payable.

EARNED INCOME AND INCOME TAXES

In addition to the various benefit options, there are two other major factors that will affect your Social Security benefits: earned income and income tax.

If you elect to start Social Security retirement benefits before reaching the FRA (as early as age sixty-two), you'll receive less benefit for each month you begin in advance. If you make your election more than thirty-six months prior to FRA, the reduction is even more significant. But if you're still working, even part time, and have opted to receive SS benefits, you're subject to an offset of any amounts earned above a limit, which is currently $17,040.

In 2017, the offset is one dollar for every two dollars earned over the limit. If you're earning over the limit, you can end up greatly reducing the amount of your SS benefit because the amount of earned income above the limit increases the offset. To top it off, your earnings are still subject to Federal Insurance Contributions Act (FICA) and Medicare employment taxes. In other words, at the same time you're receiving benefits from SS, you're also contributing to Social Security! Understanding how part-time employment can impact SS benefits prior to reaching your FRA is important. One aspect to keep in mind is working part-time still means you can earn up to the limit with no offset.

Your Social Security benefits may be subject to income tax. In fact, up to 85 percent of the benefit you receive may be taxable as ordinary income on your tax return if you exceed certain income limits. There is both a threshold amount and phase-in amount before the benefits are taxable at the 85 percent level. For married couples filing jointly, the threshold is $32,000 and is phased out at an income level of $44,000. For singles, the threshold is $25,000 and is phased out at an income of only $34,000. Therefore, if your gross income plus half of the SS benefit exceeds the threshold, then you should consider either having taxes withheld directly from the benefit amount or contributing to estimated quarterly tax payments in order to have sufficient taxes withheld. This can avoid surprises when filing your tax return the following year! Next, let's explore retirement savings and distribution plans, which include pensions, deferred annuities, individual retirement accounts (IRAs), and defined contribution plans. I'll describe each.

PENSIONS

If you're lucky enough to have a pension (which is also referred to as a defined benefit plan), then it will usually start upon retirement or by age sixty-five, if later. If you're like the majority of people transitioning into retirement and don't have a pension plan from your employer, then you may want to consider creating your own personal pension plan. You can do this by either using after-tax monies or retirement monies.

Setting up a basic personal pension plan is easy. You can start with a single premium immediate annuity (SPIA) that guarantees income to you for as long as you live. If you have a spouse, you may want to consider having your SPIA include a survivor benefit so your spouse will be eligible to receive income for the rest of his or her life. In general, I would not suggest placing all your available retirement eggs in one SPIA basket because SPIAs have no residual value and no liquidity, which means they have no transferable value upon your death, and you do not have access to the monies paid into the account once you begin receiving the annuity benefits. The bottom line is SPIAs should be considered only one part of a comprehensive retirement distribution plan.

Two types of SPIAs can be established: fixed annuity with a known amount of guaranteed income and variable, having monies invested into sub-accounts that are not guaranteed so both income and values can change. In most cases, I favor fixed SPIAs because they have lower costs compared to variable SPIAs. In addition, they come with guarantees, such as the spousal benefit I described above, and the income is guaranteed for life, regardless of how long you live!

If you started a deferred annuity while employed and want to make withdrawals upon retirement, you may be able to receive an income based upon a withdrawal percentage and potentially retain a residual value.

IRAs

Traditional, Roth, spousal, SIMPLE, SEP, inherited, and more . . . there are many different types of IRAs. In addition, there are now Roth 401(k) plans. The choices may seem overwhelming. With so many options, it's important to receive expert help if you don't know the differences between them because they can make big differences when it comes to your income taxes and distribution options.

What all IRAs share in common is you can designate a beneficiary and it will not be part of your probate estate. In addition, in many states, retirement plans are protected assets, which means they are not subject to creditors seeking to recover unpaid debts.

When deciding if you should merge different IRAs together, keep in mind that this may not be possible; each is required to retain its character. With that said, you can typically merge IRAs of the same type. For example, you can combine a rollover IRA with a traditional IRA, transfer the balance from a SEP IRA to a traditional IRA, and transfer your employer qualified plan, such as a 401(k) and 403(b), to an IRA. But you cannot combine different types of IRAs such as an inherited IRA and a traditional IRA. Even if your IRAs are eligible to be merged, doing so may not always be in your best interest. When performing a cost-benefit analysis, be sure to factor in the required distributions from each type, if any, and the amount of the taxable distribution.

In addition, each IRA has a mountain of rules and restrictions, as well as exceptions to these rules and restrictions. Most of these are set up with one goal in mind: to make sure you're paying Uncle Sam via the IRS. In this section, I'll cover the IRA points relevant to you during your retirement transition phase.

The IRS requires you to begin withdrawals by age 70½. This is referred to as the required minimum distribution, or RMD. On the other side, you are penalized for starting withdrawals from an IRA before age 59½ with one exception: You can make withdrawals before age 59½ if the amount of the withdrawal is based upon life expectancy and has substantially equal periodic payments (in other words, your payments are the same amount monthly or annually) until you reach age 59½ (this is IRS Rule 72(t), also called 72(t) election). Note that pension payments do not count as part of RMDs.

The traditional IRA is a type of investment usually accumulated with pre-tax monies. With that said, you may have made after-tax contributions to an IRA if you were not eligible to make pre-tax contributions due to exceeding an income level or already participating in a qualified retirement plan through work.

In that situation, you must keep track of the after-tax contributions so you do not pay tax on that portion of future withdrawals. These contributions are reported on your income tax return so that the IRS can keep track of the pre-tax and after-tax amounts. The good news is the after-tax contributions will come back to you tax-free.

The Roth IRA, or often referred to as simply Roth, is one of my favorite retirement products for the following three reasons: First, there is no RMD. Second, Roth IRAs are a great asset to pass to the next generation, as they are inherited income-tax free. And third, they are excellent resources for lump sum distributions in retirement because they will not impact income taxes or the Medicare premiums.

Setting up a Roth IRA is one of the best investments you can make and can be done as soon as you have earned income. Roth IRAs are even powerful investment tools for extended family members. I find them a great way to help children and grandchildren to both start saving toward the future and learn important lessons about finances. That's why they have earned my unofficial nickname, the "Grandparent Delight IRA."

Even if the minor grandchildren have earned a modest income from activities such as babysitting, mowing lawns, and lifeguarding, have them file a tax return. There will be no income tax, and it allows them to open a Roth IRA and begin the five-year clock, after which they will have access without a penalty for qualified distributions. Five years is the timeframe required from the initial opening of the account. After that time, the owner can withdraw the principal invested with no income tax liability.

There are also other circumstances where the Roth IRA can provide you access to monies before retirement. For example, homebuyers can use it to invest in their first home without penalty. They can withdraw up to $10,000.

Just like traditional IRAs, Roth IRAs have annual limits on contributions: Under age fifty, the limit is $5,500, and at age fifty or more, the limit is $6,500 per year. There are also income limits that can disqualify you from opening a Roth IRA. For singles, the phase-out is from $118,000 to $133,000, while for married couples, the phase-out is from $186,000 to $196,000.

My recommendation is that if you're eligible to establish a Roth IRA while working, then get on board! Many employer retirement plans have a Roth option in their 401(k) plan. You may also be eligible to set one up in addition to your regular employer retirement plan. If your income exceeds the maximum amount to qualify to open a Roth

IRA, you may be able to perform a Roth IRA conversion, which allows you to convert a traditional IRA into a Roth IRA. Once the conversion is in effect, you'll pay the income tax owed. In the past, the IRS has offered opportunities to do a conversion and spread the tax liability over several years. In the event this offer comes up again, I suggest you take advantage of it.

A spousal IRA allows the surviving spouse to receive the decedent's IRA with no tax on the transfer, at which point the surviving spouse may need to start RMD payments, depending upon his or her age and the age of the deceased spouse.

If someone other than the spouse is a beneficiary of an IRA, that person may open an inherited IRA, which cannot be combined with any other IRAs. A beneficiary is the person who will receive the assets in the IRA.

Inherited IRAs are helpful especially for young people who are beneficiaries because they will need to make RMDs but based upon *their* age and using the IRS Uniform Lifetime Table. As a result, the younger the beneficiary, the lower the amount of the RMD, which in turn allows the account value to grow at a greater rate. For example, let's say you are thirty-five years old, the RMD amount is 2 percent, and your total return on the IRA is 8 percent. This means that even though you took a distribution based upon the RMD, your inherited IRA grew by 6 percent!

You can have multiple inherited IRAs with different beneficiaries in order to maximize this benefit. If a group of beneficiaries is named under one IRA (for example, all children of the owner), then the oldest beneficiary's age is used to calculate the RMD. Note that the RMD is the minimum amount that must be distributed. However, beneficiaries may withdraw more if they need the additional amount for whatever purposes they choose. The amount withdrawn will be ordinary taxable income to them and reported on their individual tax return.

There are no penalties for the withdrawal, but penalties are assessed if you do not make at least the required minimum distribution. This is because the IRS does not want you to be able to continue accumulating in the inherited IRA—remember, the IRS wants your income taxes! In many cases, someone who is still working could unexpectedly move into a higher income tax bracket as a result of the added income from the required distributions of an inherited IRA.

In the appendix, you'll find a handy, quick-guide IRA chart that highlights the differences between different IRA types.

DEFINED CONTRIBUTION PLANS

These are sponsored by your employer, and the most common type is a 401(k). They may be pre- or post-tax. There is even a Roth 401(k) option that, like a Roth IRA, comprises after-tax contributions and incurs no tax on distributions.

Defined contribution plans allow for employee voluntary contributions, and most employers offer a matching contribution or profit-sharing contribution, which is tied to the amount you contribute. There are certain guidelines that employers must follow that prohibit them from discriminating against the lower income–earning staff. In order for the higher-paid employees to maximize their contributions, the employer needs to implement a safe harbor matching contribution. This is a minimum amount the employer contributes to the plan, usually with a vesting schedule, that will allow the plan to pass non-discrimination testing.

For self-employed individuals, you can set up an individual 401(k) plan that may include your spouse. This option is not available if you have employees other than your spouse.

Regardless of the type of 401(k) you have, you're subject to contribution limits. If you're under age fifty, the current maximum is $18,000 per year; if you're age fifty or older, you can contribute up to $24,000 per year.

A rollover IRA allows you to transfer your 401(k) to your own IRA when you leave the employer, at which point you can invest your IRA in a manner to your liking. Rolling over your 401(k) to an IRA is best done in a trustee-to-trustee (or direct) transfer—in other words, from the employer plan to your IRA—because it avoids the rollover rules and IRS reporting that would otherwise be required on your tax return.

In some 401(k) plans, you have an option to invest contributions into a Roth 401(k). Under such circumstances, the contributions are after tax, the withdrawals are tax-free when you reach retirement age, and there are no RMDs. The decision to make either pre-tax or after-tax contributions is dependent upon your individual situation. The younger you are, the more likely contributing to a Roth 401(k) will be beneficial because of the length of time you'll have to compound the return and you'll receive the retirement income tax-free. You can contribute to both types of 401(k)s, but you may not exceed the overall contribution limits on a combined basis.

NET UNREALIZED APPRECIATION (NUA)

When you retire from a company and consider transferring your 401(k) plan to an IRA in order to avoid paying taxes currently, there is one investment option that may exclude you from being fully taxed at ordinary tax rates: employer company stock.

Ask yourself the following: Does my 401(k) hold employer company stock?

If your answer is yes, then the IRS provides special tax treatment on these assets. This treatment is called net unrealized appreciation (NUA). You can convert your company stock from ordinary taxable income to more favorable long-term capital gains taxable income.

To take advantage of this, you must transfer the employer securities into a taxable account and not to the new IRA. This option is available only upon full termination from the retirement plan. This works especially well if the cost basis (what you paid for the shares) is very low and there is a large capital appreciation. When the securities are transferred to the taxable account, the IRS will tax the cost basis of the stock but not the appreciation portion of the securities. As a result, you can move the employer securities into the new account and then sell them paying only taxes at long-term capital gains rates on the appreciation portion, which are currently 20 percent, and not ordinary tax rates, which are currently at a maximum of 39 percent. As is always the case with the IRS, you must comply with the various tax rules that apply. But if you have employer stock in your retirement plan, be sure to determine if using the NUA option would benefit you before you make the transfer to the rollover IRA. Note that taking advantage of the NUA rules can only be done when closing out the retirement plan completely.

DISTRIBUTION PLANNING

This is by far one of the most challenging financial areas to consider during your retirement transition phase. Specifically, you have reached a point in your life where you are charged to determine how to withdraw monies from the various investment accounts that you've been diligently saving for your retirement.

Addressing the current retirement landscape requires a three-pronged approach:

1. Use more conservative projections for investment performance.
2. Have an honest conversation about saving and spending while working.
3. Create a solid spending plan when you retire.

If, during your retirement, producing the same income will require more assets, then you'll need to save more while working.

Unfortunately for many working families, saving enough to maximize the contributions to their employer retirement plan is a big struggle—let alone saving additional monies on an after-tax basis. The simple solution for those still working is to review living expenses and try to develop a plan to save first and then spend what is left over. Unfortunately, most do the opposite and therefore are unable to be prepared for retirement.

With that said, sometimes your decision has been made for you. In the case of government or corporate pensions, for example, the plans dictate when the distributions are to be made, which are usually set at a certain age or upon retirement.

Meanwhile, other types of corporate plans may include non-qualified plans, which are plans that allow the executives to defer additional earned income until retirement. These plans also have requirements as to when monies need to be distributed. Generally, the executive must withdraw the balance over a five-year period upon retirement.

But when it comes to Social Security, IRAs, 401(k)s, and other personal investment accounts, you have options that can control the timing and amounts of the distributions. For example, IRA distributions can be started any time after age 59½ and must begin no later than the year you turn age 70½.

The tricky part about distribution decisions is there is no one-size-fits-all formula that everyone can apply to his or her transition phase. Back in the old days, the advice was simple: Defer everything and withdraw from only after-tax accounts first. As much as following this recommendation is easy, it is far too simplistic for most people today. Unless, that is, you have no other choice, as would be the situation if you only have qualified retirement plans and have not saved up personal investment or savings accounts. In fact, in some cases, it may be more beneficial to start withdrawing from IRAs earlier and defer withdrawing from after-tax accounts in order to preserve access to capital without having to pay taxes each time you need money. In the end, your plan should address the needs and particular circumstances of you and your family.

Although you shouldn't follow a cookie-cutter distribution formula, you should be familiar with the following distribution fundamentals:

First, you should understand the various tax issues associated with each of your retirement distribution sources.

Second, in order to experience the lowest overall income tax liability that will meet your income needs during retirement, you want to balance your taxable income with your non-taxable or tax-favored income.

If you have pension income, it is likely 100 percent taxable and not much can be done to reduce that liability.

If you also have a personal investment portfolio that you can draw upon, you might be able to supplement the pension without significantly increasing the income taxes. Dividends and interest can be either reinvested or withdrawn, along with capital gains distributions. I like having a money market account in which the dividends and interest are deposited and the capital gains are then reinvested. This creates a cash resource to draw upon without additional tax liability that would be created if you needed to sell a position each time you wanted to make an additional withdrawal.

If you have IRAs, understanding the type of IRA and the RMD for each can also help in determining when to make withdrawals. Note that in the event you have multiple IRA accounts, you only need to make the RMD from one IRA as long as the amount of the RMD is based upon the total value of all IRA accounts.

Third, it is important to understand the Medicare premium is based upon the prior two years adjusted gross income (AGI), which is shown at the bottom of the first page of the Federal 1040 tax return. If you increase taxable distributions from retirement plans, it may impact future Medicare premiums.

As you can see, how distributions relate to your transition phase is complicated. And making the right decision about the amount of withdrawals is essential to your long-term financial wellbeing. Later in this book, I'll highlight more areas to consider, and you'll see sample tables for cash flow and investments.

RETIREMENT TIP: *my overall advice is to obtain professional help. A financial expert and an accountant will help you understand the various income tax issues associated with the timing of withdrawals from all your retirement distribution sources. As a result, you'll maximize your income and minimize taxes while preserving resources for your future financial wellness.*

Next, we'll explore estate planning, which is the final among the top retirement concerns.

CHAPTER 8

ESTATE PLANNING AND ELDER LAW

L AST, ESTATE PLANNING ROUNDED out the top-five concerns respondents had about retirement. In your case, when was the last time you reviewed your estate documents? If it has been more than five years, you should make sure they still state what you want to have happen in the event of your incapacity or demise.

If you're married, your assets are owned jointly, and each spouse is the beneficiary of the other spouse's retirement and other benefit plans. Then upon the death of one spouse, most everything would be directly transferred to the surviving spouse. Upon the survivor's death, however, these same assets may be subject to probate, incur probate cost, and require an executor to administer the distribution of the assets under a will. An executor is the person named in your will who is charged with implementing the distributions and other requests that are outlined in the will.

EXECUTOR CAVEATS

If you're married, you have a will, and you've named your spouse as the executor, what happens if he or she is unable to carry out the duties of the executor? For example, what if your spouse is ill or mentally incapacitated? This is where a successor executor would step in or where a successor trustee would be appointed.

Upon your passing, many issues must be addressed in a timely manner, and the person named in the will is responsible to make sure all tasks are taken care of. That is why it may not always be the best idea to name your spouse as the executor; he or she may be incapacitated or too emotionally distraught after your passing to carry out the long list of probate items. If you do not have a will, then you have to file intestate, requiring you to go to the court of wills and obtain the proper documents to have a person appointed as the executor or the courts may appoint someone of their choosing. A basic will is a necessity, especially when there are minor children involved, as the court will appoint a guardian if you have not done so in a will. This creates additional cost and can delay the distribution of assets to the beneficiaries.

EXECUTOR CHECKLIST

Being an executor is often a time-consuming responsibility. As mentioned, having your spouse listed as the executor in your will or as a successor trustee in your revocable trusts can be a major problem if the spouse is also aging and may not be capable of dealing with all the necessary issues that come with the responsibilities of the position. When you are younger, this does not appear to be as much of an issue; however, in retirement, it can become a major problem. Be sure to review all estate documents to be sure that the persons identified as executor or successor trustee are willing and able to carry out the tasks of the position. (In the appendix, I have listed the duties of the executor to give an idea of the responsibilities you are placing on that person.)

Note that many of these tasks may benefit from professional help in order to avoid errors and potential penalties. As someone who provides estate-planning expertise to my clients every day, I can attest to how overwhelming playing this executor role can be. In my own family's case, my oldest sister was designated executor of my father's estate after he passed. My parents assumed that as the oldest child and a successful attorney, my sister would be the best qualified to be the executor. But after my dad's death, my sister let me know she didn't want to play the role that was outlined in his will. Unfortunately, my parents never bothered asking her if she even wanted to assume the immense responsibility.

"Stan, I'm a lawyer in the Treasury Department. I don't have a clue about estates," she told me.

Because of my experience in dealing with the financial matters in estates, my sister asked me to take on the task for both my father's estate and my mother's estate when that time came. I knew how much responsibility it was, and I agreed to be the executor. To my sister's relief, my mom and my other sisters went along with the decision.

In this section, I'll address some of the more common types of estate documents that may benefit your overall retirement planning: will, advanced medical directive (AMD), durable power of attorney (POA), revocable living trust, and special needs trust (SNT).

Keep in mind this is intended to provide introductory information and is by no means a substitute for legal advice. Just as I advise my clients, I recommend you consult with an estate tax or elder law attorney in your jurisdiction to receive proper advice on the specific types of estate documents you need to address your particular situation.

Will: This is the most common estate document. It can take care of transferring assets to the survivor and other beneficiaries. It is also the document used for identifying the guardians of minor children. If no guardian is chosen, then the court will appoint one for you and it may not be your best choice. For most retirees, the needs of minor children are not an issue. With that said, there are situations in which an adult child who is disabled is living with aging parents. These individuals may have care requirements that must continue even after parents are no longer able to care for them.

When drafting your will, designating an executor is an important step. This person will manage the estate through probate and make the distributions as outlined under the will's terms. This can be a very time-consuming and often frustrating experience. For proof, just look at the bulleted executor task checklist in this chapter! And as I've explained, spouses may not be the best choice here. In these instances, I often recommend my clients designate a co-executor (which is not the same as a successor), such as another family member, or a qualified individual, such as an attorney or a trust company, to be the party assigned to take on this responsibility. I generally recommend a professional be named successor for the executor or trustee (the person assigned to handle trust issues) in the event a family member is unable to perform the duties and carry out the terms of the document. A successor is the person or entity that takes over for existing trustees or executors when they are no longer able to do the job.

Advance Medical Directives (AMD): These may include a durable power of attorney (POA) for healthcare and a living will. The POA appoints another person, called an agent, to make the healthcare decisions in the event you are incapacitated. The living will is a document that expresses your wishes concerning end-of-life decisions if you're unable to communicate your intentions—this is the "pull the plug" document and may include instructions for medication and when to provide or withhold medical treatments that could prolong life unnecessarily. This is sometimes referred to as having a DNR or "do not resuscitate" in the medical file. Technically, the DNR is a separate document and MUST be signed by the individual's doctor. The AMD can give the agent the authority to sign a DNR on behalf of the patient.

Durable Power of Attorney (POA): This is a document that enables one person to act on behalf of another in dealing with financial matters. It may or may not require a medical condition or physician's letter stating incapacity to trigger the date it becomes effective, or it may be a limited power, restricted to a specific action.

Keep in mind that if you provide a general POA to someone without restrictions, that person could act on your behalf at any time, regardless of your health! When deciding whom to give POA, make sure you select an individual that is good with money; if your prospective POA designee cannot balance his or her own checkbook, how will this person keep your finances in order?

Revocable Living Trust: The purpose of this document is to allow your beneficiaries to receive assets upon your death without going through probate. As a result, your beneficiaries save executor fees and probate costs. In many instances, it also allows the transfer of assets to occur without delay. The "revocable" part of the living trust means it can be amended at any time by the trust's grantor, which is the person that created the trust. A revocable living trust does not become irrevocable until the grantor's death.

During your lifetime, you are acting as your trust's trustee. Only in the event of your incapacity or death will the successor trustee step in to manage the trust assets. It is important for the trust to specifically state the trustee's authority. A common item inadvertently not stated in a trust is the ability to make charitable contributions.

In addition, make sure the revocable living trust spells out how and when the successor trustee(s) will step in to represent your wishes. Contrary to popular belief, a letter from a physician may not always be necessary.

Last, assets transferred by trust are private in the sense that the estate is not made public, and no public records are required. With a probate estate, the court of wills retains estate records, which are available to the public. A revocable trust uses the grantor's Social Security number while he or she is alive. After death, the successor trustee will need to obtain a new tax identification number from the IRS.

Special Needs Trust (SNT): This trust is used to protect the individual's ability to obtain means-based public benefits and entitlement programs from the government such as Supplemental Security Income (SSI), Social Security disability benefits, and Medicare or Medicaid. If a disabled person inherits assets, those assets must be spent down before he or she becomes eligible to receive SSI or Medicaid benefits or both. The SNT can hold assets and supplement the government benefits without jeopardizing those benefits. In order to properly draft your legal documents, I recommend you work with an attorney with a background in SNTs.

AVOIDING PROBATE

In many jurisdictions, probate is not as costly as it once was. While the expense may not be as exorbitant anymore, what still remains is the nightmare of dealing with the mountains of administration and red tape. The time required to process the estate through probate is reason alone to avoid it. Here are some common ways people steer clear of probate:

- **Joint ownership with right of survivorship:** Upon the death of one partner, the other retains the asset. Upon the other's death, the asset may then need to go through probate.

- **Life insurance proceeds paid via a beneficiary designation:** As long as you are not naming the estate as a beneficiary, the death benefit will pass directly to the named beneficiary with no income tax and no probate.

- **Transfer on death (TOD) or pay on death (POD) registration:** These act similar to having a named beneficiary, except the accounts are investments or bank accounts and not insurance or retirement accounts.

- **Lifetime gifts:** When these are made to any person within the annual gift exclusion, they will reduce the amount of probate assets.

- **Revocable and irrevocable trusts**: A revocable trust is used during a person's lifetime. Think of it as a bucket. Because it has no lid, things can be added and removed at any time as long as the assets are registered in the name of the trust. Items such as investments, bank accounts, cars, and even your house can be registered or titled in the name of the trust. Upon the death of the grantor or trustor, the trust becomes irrevocable and receives a separate tax entity requiring a tax ID number.

  But if the person becomes incapacitated, the successor trustee takes over and manages the person's affairs on his or her behalf. This is one of the most important benefits of having a revocable living trust. Note that such trusts can hold assets from different jurisdictions so that an estate will not have to file in different states upon the death of the grantor.

  An irrevocable trust is created when a person wants to remove an asset from his or her estate or preserve assets for an intended beneficiary such as a special needs child. Life insurance used to be one of the primary assets held in irrevocable trust to avoid having the death benefit included in one's estate for estate tax purposes. But with the new estate tax laws now in place, this is not necessary unless you are one of the one percenters with estate assets over twelve million dollars.

THE ROLE OF ELDER LAW ATTORNEYS

Elder law attorneys have broad expertise that includes overall estate planning, along with life care and end-of-life planning. They work collaboratively with your other advisers such as your financial and insurance professionals.

Elder law attorneys serve as your legal advocate and help coordinate all the various services, benefits, and protections you'll most likely need as you age. This may include complex estate planning, as well as providing expertise regarding LTC whether aging in place or in a care facility. In addition, many elder law attorneys will work with clients dealing with an incapacitated spouse or special needs child.

The following are services an elder law attorney may provide:

- Estate planning and trust administration
- LTC planning
- SNT planning
- Life care planning
- Guardianship
- Protecting your home from creditors
- Maximizing public assistance and government entitlement benefits

As you've read, you have many options in regard to your estate planning. Effective estate planning has the goal of protecting your assets, reducing estate tax, transferring costs, and allowing your wishes to be carried out in the event of either your incapacity or death. When your assets are subject to estate taxes, you'll require more advanced estate planning. With that said, less than 1 percent of the population is affected under current estate tax laws.

If you take seriously your long-term retirement planning, some or all of the top-five retirement concerns will resonate with you.

Now that we've set the retirement stage and you've learned about retirees' main concerns, you have the foundation necessary to apply this information to the next section. In part 3, we'll explore the five stages of retirement.

PART THREE
The 5 Stages of Retirement

In part 3, you'll learn about the highs and lows you'll experience over the next years and decades. From the freedom of leading a life where work becomes optional to taking care of your needs up to the very end, you'll gain insight into the challenges that lie ahead and how to address them skillfully. Remember, the goal is to live your one best retirement life. The stages are as follows:

1. Transitioning

2. Go-Go Years

3. Slow-Go Years

4. No-Go Years

5. The Exit

In the next chapter, we'll begin with the first one: transitioning.

CHAPTER 9
TRANSITIONING

Fully preparing to transition into my retirement was
much more challenging than I had thought, but after all
the work, I'm now much happier and really enjoying all
that retirement offers to us and our family.

– *Survey respondent*

MELISSA IS A CLIENT I had worked with for many years. She followed my recommendations, and as a result, she transitioned smoothly into retirement. During one of our follow-up meetings about six months after Melissa retired, she described how she went to her favorite department store to buy a new outfit for a trip.

At the cash register, the attendant offered her a 20 percent discount on her purchases that day if she signed up for the store's credit card. Melissa made wise financial decisions and believed she would benefit from enrolling.

"I began filling out the application," she told me. "And once I reached the lines that asked for my employment and income, I just stared at them, uncertain what to write."

She had not fully absorbed her new identity as a retiree, and the fact she didn't know how to answer the employment and income questions made this clear to her.

"It took me over a year after I left work to get used to the retirement label," she said.

HOW DO YOU FEEL AT THIS POINT IN YOUR LIFE?

Based on the survey results as well as my work advising men and women during the transition phase, I've noticed two trends. Let's call them a tale of two retirees.

In the first group are high-income earners. These include lawyers, doctors, corporate executives, and business owners.

In the second group are blue-collar to middle white-collar employees. These include middle management employees, self-employed family business owners, and people working in the trades such as plumbers, electricians, and building contractors.

Without accounting for income or the size of a nest egg, if I were to ask you, "Which group has a tougher emotional time with retirement?" would you select group one or group two?

Experience has taught me that despite the significant amount of retirement savings high-income earners have, they often find themselves at an existential crossroads.

My theory about this has to do with what individuals based their identity on. For people who attached a large part of their identity to their job title and status, suddenly losing both can be a shock to the system. No doubt, there are plenty of people who don't earn six or seven figures and fall into a retirement funk, but the trend lines I've seen among high-income earners in positions of power and prestige are pretty consistent. Saying the words, "I'm retired," can feel like the end of their lives as they've known them. They may feel like they have left their reputations and brains back at the office and are frustrated with starting over.

On the other hand, I've noticed that group two often transitions into retirement with fewer of the mental hang-ups than group one. Perhaps this is because they've derived less of their identity in their job title and more of it in other aspects of their lives.

Many in group two celebrate the freedom after decades of hard work and are thrilled to hit the road in their RV. This tale of two retirees makes an important point: Regardless of where you land on the income spectrum, retirement requires planning to live rather than planning to stop working.

The following is a sample of insights respondents provided me that relate to retirement's Transitioning stage:

- It took me weeks to finally get out of the house.

- I woke up and stared at a blank screen on my computer. I always had a full schedule, and now the calendar is empty.

- Is there such a thing as too much golf?

- I need structure and purpose

- Having the best time of my life. Wish I had made the decision to retire much earlier.

- I miss my work and my colleagues.

- How did I ever get anything done before?

- I can't believe how old people my age are!

Do some of these comments reflect how you're feeling at this stage of your life?

It is not at all uncommon for newly retired individuals to feel very lost or anxious during this initial stage. No longer receiving a regular paycheck and trying to fill the void of working is very challenging. For many others, it can be a feeling of loss, and they may need to go through a grieving period, which can occur anytime we leave someone or something behind. But proper guidance and connecting with family and friends who have already made the transition and done it well can be very beneficial.

As with most of life's changes, it takes time to make the adjustment. In the end, after you figure out how to no longer depend on having to make a living as you did throughout most of your adulthood, I think you'll find greater happiness in being able to be in control of your life.

Successfully moving through this stage isn't easy, and it will require work on your part—as the survey respondent at the beginning described and as you'll discover as you read through this stage. But once you complete the necessary tasks that are part of a Real Retirement Plan, you'll be able to enjoy the life you envisioned. In this section, you'll learn the first five retirement transition tasks.

THE FIRST FIVE STEPS YOU MUST TAKE

1. Have open and honest conversations with your spouse or partner about your retirement journey

If you haven't completed the Retirement Expectations Exercise that appears in appendix D yet, now is the time. Having an honest conversation with your spouse or partner about how you envision your retirement, including each of your greatest concerns, fears, desires, and wants, is an essential step during this stage.

2. Form a team of professionals that will provide you guidance

Once you realize that the nest egg you've created—based on all your dreams, plans, and savings to this point—will be significantly affected by decisions you now make, you may also realize you cannot go it alone—even if you've gone it alone up to this point. The reason is that everything you know or think you know is about to change!

As far as couples transitioning into retirement are concerned, as someone who's evaluated people's financial lives for his entire career, I can confidently say that in most instances, one spouse has a better grasp of the couple's finances than the other. And often the knowledge gap is huge. In other words, one spouse knows everything about the couple's financials, and other person is essentially financially illiterate.

If the spouse with the high level of financial knowledge outlives his or her partner, this will most likely result in a financially smooth transition from partnership to singlehood. But if the spouse with less or no financial knowledge outlives his or her partner, this could result in stress and needlessly losing money as a result of poor decision-making. *So, if you're the one who has been mostly on the sidelines managing your family financial affairs, it's time to get up and get into the game.*

Even among financially savvy couples, forming a team is usually a good idea. This group of professionals includes some or all of the following: estate or elder law attorney, CFP, CPA, banker, and insurance agent. A combination of these experts will best serve your long-term interests. By bringing them onto your team, they will play an essential role in developing your Real Retirement Plan. You'll leverage their expertise in order to help you make better and more informed decisions that may affect you, your spouse or partner, and future generations.

In regard to the financial expert who is part of your team, I recommend hiring one with a Certified Financial Planner (CFP) designation. As a financial expert who chose to earn the CFP title because I believed in the organization's training, continuing education, fiduciary responsibility, and code of ethics, I'm a strong supporter of the CFP designation. CFPs are trained in playing a central role coordinating the other members of your team. Think of a CFP as a coach who makes sure the game plan is solid and then works with team members to ensure the plan is monitored, revised, and maintained in order to accomplish your overall goals and wishes now and after you pass away.

3. Keep family informed of your plans

A key component of a Real Retirement Plan is to involve your family as you develop and implement it. This will increase the likelihood that your wishes will be met, your family members will act in your best interest, and you'll avoid conflicts among family members when you need their help the most. Keeping your family informed can be as simple as asking the person you wish to be the executor or successor trustee if he or she will, in fact, want to serve in that capacity.

As you've read previously, I'm a strong believer in family meetings in instances when you know you and your estate will benefit from them. During a family meeting, you'll inform your loved ones of your intentions and inform everyone of who has been designated as the executor or trustee. In addition, you'll point out if you have any special provisions for one person, such as a child who may be incapacitated or one who has chosen to be in a career (charitable, religious, or other type) that does not provide an opportunity to create a sustainable financial wellness. And if you have charities you are supporting, you may need to identify them and how you wish to help them upon your death. If you're concerned about maintaining your privacy, a family meeting doesn't require you to hand out your financial statements or disclose all your intentions in your will. In other words, you can make the family meeting reflect your values and preferences.

A NOTE TO PARENTS OF ADULT CHILDREN: *When possible, consider informing your sons and daughters about your financial situation and estate plans because, in many cases, this discussion will reduce their fear and anxiety associated with how best to care for you in the future.*

This does not have to be a large family meeting. It can be an informational talk with the people you've designated as executor or successor trustee or given medical power of attorney or financial power of attorney. In instances where an honest conversation is possible, involving your children is an important step because they will likely be the ones who will manage your affairs when you're no longer able and will end up performing or overseeing most of the care. In instances where the elderly husband becomes incapacitated, if the wife is physically able, she may take on the burden of care.

In many other cases, however, if one or more adult daughters in the family live close enough to provide consistent oversight, their parents often designate them to be in charge of their care when the need arises. If an elderly couple or individual has no adult children or they live far away, then these parents will most likely hire people to manage their care at home or within a care facility.

A NOTE TO ADULT CHILDREN OF AGING PARENTS: *Many times, my clients have told me, "Stan, my parents don't want to talk about their finances or estate planning. When I've brought the subject up, they became annoyed verging on downright anger."*

Here's where working with a financial adviser will benefit you. He or she can play the bad guy or gal. For instance, I've told my clients to say the following to their parents: "I've been working with a financial adviser to build a long-term plan. He [or she] needs some information about your financial situation in order to see if it will impact my own plan."

When speaking with aging parents, the key to a successful conversation—one that benefits you and your parents—is maintaining skillful delivery. If your goal is to understand their wishes and financial state, then think through your conversation beforehand instead of improvising and hoping for the best.

Rather than focus your conversation on having them tell you about their personal finances, concentrate on exploring their intentions for their retirement and, specifically, what they would like done if one or both of them became incapacitated.

By taking this approach, you'll increase the likelihood your parents will understand you have their best interest at heart and that you aren't probing into their lives because you're nosey or greedy or both. With their defenses softened, this may lead to a broader and more candid discussion about their estate and long-term care plans, and how they have prepared for the future.

ONE OTHER NOTE ABOUT AGING PARENTS: *You may think that they should be investing differently, especially if they are not getting the kinds of returns you are getting on your portfolio. Just take a step back and realize that the portfolio may not need to be getting the higher rate of return as asset protection may be more important than asset appreciation to them. If their needs are being met and they are financially stable, then their financial portfolio should not be an issue. Remember that their interpretation of risk and yours may not be the same!*

4. Update financial statements yearly

Having up-to-date financial statements is an effective way to level the knowledge playing field between couples. If your spouse is less informed about your combined financial status, reviewing financial statements with him or her is an effective way to begin the education process. A good time to do this is when you file your tax returns because this is when you'll have compiled the majority of your important financial documents in one place.

While you're having financial conversations with your significant other, tax season is also a good time to keep your family informed of any major changes to your retirement plan. Many people are uncomfortable having these conversations with family members. But let me assure you, even if you're not talking about your financial situation with them, they are certainly talking about it amongst themselves!

So rather than have them base their conclusions on speculation and conjecture, I recommend giving them the facts if your family dynamic allows this level of communication. You should also keep them informed of any medical changes that may affect your retirement plans.

As you progress through the retirement stages, your concerns about having enough resources to provide for your long-term needs will most likely increase. I recall one client telling me, "My dad didn't expect to live this long, and now he's worried about running out of money!"

By obtaining and reviewing your financial statements regularly as time passes, you'll have the information necessary to make wise course corrections, which will allow you to prepare for the future more effectively than would otherwise be the case.

Last, check your information held by the major credit bureaus annually. From foreign hacking to stolen credit cards, personal identity data breaches are part of modern life and are often out of our control. What we can control, however, is our vigilance over our prized personal identities and credit. To avoid the headaches related to identify fraud, obtain your free annual report that will alert you of any issues that may need to be resolved, and sign up for identity-theft protection; the cost of enrolling is worth the peace of mind and the services you'll receive.

5. Update estate documents at least every five years

As you read previously, hiring an attorney to draft an estate plan is one of the preliminary steps in the estate-planning process. Laws and your personal circumstances are always changing, and you need to be on top of any issues that may affect your estate plans. In addition, unlike a trust, powers of attorney and medical directives have a shelf life, so they need to be updated and re-signed in order for them to be valid at the time you need them.

Now that you've learned about the first five steps to take, you're ready for the next one. A fundamental part of a Real Retirement Plan is to identify where your money is going.

NEXT STEP: CREATE A RETIREMENT SPENDING PLAN

Without an accurate accounting of your expenses, you cannot create a reliable spending plan for your retirement years.

A spending plan reflects all current living expenses that you divide into several categories—essential recurring monthly, non-recurring, and voluntary (or discretionary)—which will allow you to plan to splurge once in a while.

- Essential recurring monthly living expenses include mortgage, rent, food, utilities, health insurance, prescriptions, and auto expenses; in other words, bills for purchases and services you need each month.

- Non-recurring expenses comprise what you need to pay on a quarterly, semi-annual, or annual basis. They may include things such as home, auto, life, and LTC insurance premiums; real estate taxes; and quarterly estimated income taxes. These may also include unexpected expenses such as hospital stays, other types of family emergencies, or home repair, as when the heater needs replacement or the roof leaks.

- Voluntary or discretionary expenses include entertainment, clothing, vacations, your next car (which may be your last!), spoiling grandkids, elective home improvement, and other indulgences.

Nowadays, you have many reliable resources to help you identify your living expenses. Most banks provide a cash flow tool or budget program that allows you to review a monthly summary of expenses. This summary may help you develop a spending plan. Most banks also have online bill pay options. I highly encourage my clients to sign up for these services because they help manage cash flow and provide useful reports showing your spending in various categories. Also, from groceries and clothes to filling up the car with gas, many people use a credit card to make their purchases. One benefit of paying with plastic is that your credit card company most likely provides a summary of expenses broken down into various categories.

Consider purchasing bookkeeping software, such as Quicken, which can be linked to your bank account and provide you with many automated options to create an income and cash flow analysis. It's critical to understand not just where your money is coming from but also where it's going! Managing expenses will better enable you to sustain your long-term financial situation. Having a solid spending plan in place can allay the fear of running out of money before you run out of time.

A LEGACY IDEA FOR GRANDPARENTS

Based on what experience in my financial advisory years has shown me, grandparents love to spoil their grandchildren, have fun with them, and allow them to do many things that would otherwise raise an eyebrow from their parents. So, as grandparents, you get to spoil the grandkids and then hand them back to their parents for discipline—you're experiencing the best of both worlds! Here are a few tips that may have lasting impact on your grandchildren and please their parents.

If you 're fortunate enough to have assets you don't need, consider involving the grandkids in building their own small investment nest egg by gifting up to fifteen thousand dollars per year directly to them (the maximum annual gift tax exclusion, that is, the maximum amount you can give to each person for which the recipient owes no tax to the IRS). Currently this gift has no adverse tax consequences for you or them!

If the grandkids are under age eighteen, I suggest opening a Uniform Transfers to Minors Trust (UTMA) or Uniform Gifts to Minors (UGMA) registration. State rules determine which of the two is available—UTMA has replaced UGMA for most (but not all) states—and some states have special provisions under UTMA. These monies are considered a "completed" gift to the child. Completed means the child now owns the monies gifted even though he or she may not have access to them until age eighteen or twenty-one, depending upon the state regulations. Maybe the kids would like to buy stocks of companies they know from using their products like Apple, Microsoft, Disney, Facebook, or Walmart. Or consider simply setting them up with a broad index such as the S&P 500.

Another idea I mentioned earlier is to help grandchildren open a Roth IRA once they have earned income. You can encourage them to save by offering to match any amount they contribute on their own. These accounts can be opened with as little as $250 with most mutual funds, and you can make additional contributions with as little as $25.

Do you want to help in funding your grandchildren's college educations? It's easy to set up a 529 College Savings Plan in most states, and you may even be eligible to receive a tax deduction on your state tax return! If a 529 College Savings Plan is not available in your state, you can open one in another state. Unfortunately, by doing so you will not benefit from a state tax deduction. Also, note that if you have grandchildren entering college, you can pay tuition directly to the educational institution and it will not count toward the annual gift tax exclusion limitation.

I also recommend involving your grandkids in charitable ventures such as helping out at homeless shelters or food banks or preparing meals for elderly or homeless people. This will serve as a memorable opportunity to share time with the grandkids and instill some of your values into them.

Next, consider the iconic lemonade stand! Kids as young as five years old can set up a little business by their home to sell fresh lemonade. This can be a lucrative venture on hot summer days. Keep in mind doing so requires supervision and assistance from parents or grandparents or both.

When it comes to technology, kids today have many more skills from all the cutting-edge innovations they've been exposed to at such early ages. You may find they can teach you new tricks as well. My suggestion is if you're lucky enough to have grandkids, then get involved in their lives and learn from one another. Your investment in their lives may be one of the most memorable times of your life.

One of my clients told me that he made an effort to sometimes read the same books and listen to the same music that his grandkids did. That way, he would be able to stay in tune with the tastes and trends of the younger generation and better relate with his grandkids. He would also enlist his grandkids to help him with his electronic devices such as downloading apps on his smartphone and tablet.

DIFFICULT TRANSITIONS:
SMALL BUSINESS OWNERS AND CORPORATE EXECUTIVES

The retirement transition phase often poses challenges and difficulties for business owners and corporate executives. If you're one of these individuals, you're in a unique situation when it comes to negotiating the financial and other benefits you'll obtain once you exit your business. If done unwisely, your exit can present conflicts that can negatively affect your overall retirement objectives.

For example, let's say you're a small business owner. You've built a successful company that has allowed you to provide for your family. Now that you're transitioning into retirement, you're charged to figure out your future as well as your business's future. Will you pass your business down to the next generation or sell it to a competitor or loyal employee?

You must also ask yourself: Does the business have transferrable value? In other words, will a buyer be willing to pay you a fair market value for your business beyond inventory or book value?

If you plan to pass your business to a new owner, rarely does he or she hand you stacks of bills, and you simply walk out the door with your suitcase full of cash. Instead, a successful transfer between owners requires an agreement spelling out how the purchase will be completed. Also, your buyer will most likely seek assurance that once he or she takes ownership, the business will continue to generate revenue and the buyer will retain your client base.

As a result, most small business purchases include a combination of a down payment, promissory notes or bank loans, and an earn-out period, which adjusts the purchase amount based on a specified retention rate of clients or a specified amount of earnings after a set period (usually one to three years).

In the event the new owner of your business is a son or daughter, then you have another set of problems to consider. As I've seen with my business-owner clients, their hopes of carefree days without the day-to-day burdens of business ownership are frequently dashed once they find themselves continually involved in the business that the next generation is now ostensibly managing.

In other instances, the parent-owner has difficulty letting go and hangs around the business. He or she can make comments such as, "That's not the way I did things for all those years," to express disapproval of new decisions. Behavior from passive-aggressive to the outright rejection of how the new owner is managing the business can create conflict between parents and their children.

In and of themselves, wise exit strategies for small business owners could fill a book. The complexity of the subject explains why nearly 90 percent of US small businesses do not stay afloat after the owner has retired or died.

As far as executives are concerned, many have employment agreements that spell out exit strategies. Many also contain language that will adjust the exit payout amount based on performance. In addition, the payout may be in cash, notes, company stock, or any combination of these. If you retire prior to age sixty-five, the agreement may include a continuation of benefits for a specified time for health, dental, vision, or any combination of these.

Whether you are a business owner or corporate executive, the results of retirement negotiations can have a big impact on your expected lifestyle. The more clearly you understand how to transition your small business or solidify the executive agreement wisely, the better you'll be prepared for your long-term retirement.

TWO WHAT–IF SCENARIOS
DURING TRANSITION INTO RETIREMENT

Abe and Barbara: Looking Abroad

Some retirees realize they may experience a drop in income that may limit their retirement options. They find themselves asking, "What if I can't afford to live where I am right now?" In order to address this concern, they've decided to move—not just to another city or state but to another country.

Let's imagine that rather than a textbook-perfect retirement scenario, a married couple, Abe and Barbara, were transitioning into retirement and their assets were lower than they wished to have. In fact, each had gone through nasty divorces in their mid-forties. Together they managed to accumulate about $900,000 in retirement assets, another $250,000 in after-tax accounts, but had no pensions. They also had about $300,000 in their home equity. This was their best-case scenario after scrimping and saving all they could.

Abe and Barbara were adventurous souls and remained open to multiple options. They sought comfort and security in their retirement years and wanted to be able to travel in the United States and other countries. They also wanted to be in a place where they could easily be with the kids and grandkids and their family members could easily visit them. After years of living in Michigan, they wanted to move to a warmer climate where they wouldn't have to deal with brutal winters anymore. While there were certainly warmer-climate options domestically, the couple thought many of them were "elephant burial grounds," as they liked to call them, where retirees went to die. That didn't interest them.

Barbara had spent hours researching retirement options online, investigating living outside the United States, and paging through *International Living* magazine. Based on her studies, she had found many countries close to the United States that were safe, friendly to US residents, and had a much lower cost of living than where they lived. In fact, many of these countries welcomed US retirees (and their pocketbooks) and made meeting residency requirements easy.

They used the following checklist to perform their research in order to narrow down their options:

- **Healthcare:** Was a healthcare system available, how good was it, and would their insurance cover the cost of the healthcare? What additional vaccines would be necessary, and what types of illnesses might be encountered that were not common in the United States?

- **Safety:** Was the country they were considering a stable government, and did it have a low level of crime?

- **Property taxes:** What were the taxes in the country, and would they be subject to additional taxes as expats? They found that some countries taxed the belongings that were brought into the country every year! They learned that this was a way to discourage transporting things that could be purchased within the country.

- **Income taxes:** How would their retirement income be taxed by the United States and the resident country?

- **Travel:** What documents would be needed, and would they be able to travel within the country freely as well as travel back and forth between the country and the United States easily?

- **Cost of living and currency:** What exactly was the cost of living needed to meet their lifestyle? Would the country accept US dollars, and were the exchange rates stable?

- **Language:** Would they need to learn the language, or were the citizens bilingual?

- **Community and social life:** Were there areas that had a large population of other expats? Did the area offer the types of entertainment and social events they were looking for?

- **Activities:** Did the area have access to such things as tennis, golf, boating, hiking, swimming, and parks? How close were metropolitan communities? What was the country best known for globally?

- **Food:** Were there any dietary issues with available food sources?

- **Housing:** What types of housing were available, and were they near the resources that were most important to their needs, wishes, wants, and desires?

- **Due diligence**: What are the impressions from actually exploring the places several times, each time for at least a week?

After narrowing down their list, Abe and Barbara made several trips south to visit the areas—both with a real estate agent and on their own. After an exhaustive search, Abe and Barbara chose Panama in Central America. They understood why it rated so high on the 2017 Annual Global Retirement Index. Much of the revenue from the country's famous canal is reinvested into Panama's infrastructure, which likely contributes to its long history of political stability and openness to foreign residents. Because of the country's popularity, real estate prices appear to be on the rise, which meant if the couple decided to move again, they felt they could easily sell their home.

The US dollar is Panama's currency, and the pervasive use of English clinched the decision. Abe and Barbara looked forward to having friends and relatives visit them in their exotic and beautiful retirement home on the Pacific Ocean. And their Midwest family members and friends were thrilled with escaping Michigan winters and visiting them in tropical Panama.

ONE WORD OF CAUTION: *Instability in a foreign country can mean you leave with the clothes on your back, so be sure to do your homework before making such a life-changing decision.*

Jim and Carol: Inheritance Surprise

As Jim and Carol were working closely with their financial advisor to develop their retirement plan, Jim revealed he was expecting to receive an inheritance once his parents died. This was prior to his father's cancer diagnosis.

Fortunately, treating the aggressive stomach cancer extended his father's life. However, Jim's father spent the last six months of his life in a care facility, and his mother ended up living in an assisted care facility nearby.

The massive medical bills for his long-term care needs exceeded the couple's financial resources and left almost no estate for his parents to transfer to Jim.

As a result, Jim had to make significant adjustments to his own retirement plans, now that he could not depend upon his anticipated inheritance. He ended up continuing to work until he was seventy instead of his original plan of retiring early at age sixty-two.

Jim's predicament points to two diametrically opposed scenarios I've often seen among my clients—men and women who have been shocked with joy after receiving money they didn't expect or shocked with horror after finding out they wouldn't receive a penny. I always recommend NOT counting on an inheritance and, instead, planning for your retirement based on your own resources. The sole exception is if there is an irrevocable trust with the money designated to you already in it to provide an additional resource at your own retirement.

How could Jim's parents have planned to leave a financial legacy even if they spent down their assets? They could have done so by setting up a permanent life insurance policy that would pay the benefits upon the surviving parent's death. This is called last-survivor life insurance. In that way, the value of the tax-free insurance proceeds could have provided the legacy they wanted, even when they had spent down most of their other assets for their long-term care needs. In addition, they would have benefited greatly from having an LTC policy for both that would have reduced the drawdown of their financial assets.

LIVING WELL DURING YOUR TRANSITION INTO RETIREMENT

It is not just about surviving in retirement; it is about living life well.
– *Survey Respondent*

With medical advances and healthier lifestyles, we're living longer than ever. But for many of us, quality is just as important as quantity. If our futures will extend decades after the retirement transition phase, how do we want to spend them? If you're like me, experiencing happiness is high on your list.

Our environments play a large role in our sense of wellbeing. If we're surrounded by positive, happy people, they will influence our own happiness. If we're surrounded by negative, unhappy people, developing our own happiness becomes an uphill battle. So, have fun and be around others who enjoy life.

My sister lost her husband and was left a widow in retirement. While part of her wanted to sulk in her loss, she realized the futility in sitting in a recliner watching the years pass. Rather than witness the world go by without her, she decided to jump in and be part of the fun. She started traveling with friends and by herself, taking adventures she never thought she would.

She realized there was life after a spouse's death. In fact, she knew her husband would have encouraged her to find happiness during her retirement years.

The top five retirement concerns combined with the information you've read about in this stage demonstrate the immense responsibilities required to transition well into retirement. In fact, based on what countless clients have told me over the nearly four decades I've worked as a financial adviser, this stage of life is one of the most significant and challenging you'll ever go through.

Planning and addressing what I've covered in preparing to live well in retirement may not make it to the top of your to-do list right now. No doubt, the immense responsibilities of daily life often leave us busy and maybe even overwhelmed. But retiring well, in other words, avoiding the Thelma and Louise and Bonnie and Clyde Plans you read about earlier, requires focus and time.

For those with few assets, you may be tempted to pull the financial and estate planning version of Thelma and Louise. But don't despair. I assure you that you have options. For starters, take your foot off the gas pedal. Next, talk to an elder law attorney that specializes in LTC and Medicaid. This expert will help you obtain all the public benefits available to you and your family.

For those of you with a larger estate, you are charged with the responsibility to protect it by leveraging all the tools you've read about that apply to your circumstances. Doing so is the key to navigating the retirement transition phase successfully. I can assure you that, whether your retirement transition phase can afford you membership into an exclusive golf club or you must clip coupons every month to pay the bills, what you've read so far applies to you.

As the saying goes, "Failing to plan is planning to fail." Every minute you spend using this stage to guide your planning will move you away from driving off a cliff and toward protecting your estate and your emotional and physical wellbeing as you age. And knowing you've done your best to protect yourself and those you care about most is the difference between stress that keeps you up and night and peace of mind beyond words.

CHAPTER 10

GO-GO YEARS

The life expectancy of a healthy sixty-five-year-old is 20.4 years.
– *IRS Unified Life Expectancy Tables*

ROBERT AND SARA MET me in my office for one of our regular client meetings. During our previous appointment, I had provided them the Retirement Expectations Exercise questions (see appendix D). I had instructed them to respond to the survey separately and then come together and share their answers with each other. The present meeting's agenda included reviewing how the exercise went for them.

"Stan, I think we'd have been better off if we'd never done the exercise," Sara said.

By the stressed look on Robert's face, I could tell he agreed.

"Why?" I asked.

"It all started once we began sharing our answers. After nearly an hour of heated discussion, we hadn't even gotten past question four!" she said.

For review, the first four questions of the Retirement Expectations Exercise are as follows:

- What are your vision and personal expectations in retirement?

- What is on your bucket list?

- What are your biggest concerns for this period of your life?

- What activities have you talked about doing but never found the time to do before while working?

The couple, who had been married nearly all their adult lives, explained to me that when they heard each other's responses to the first four questions, they wondered if they even knew each other anymore.

For example, the first item on Robert's bucket list was to take a long cruise down the intercostal waterway from the Chesapeake Bay to Key West. Meanwhile, on Sara's bucket list, her first item was to move closer to the grandchildren. Robert wanted to travel as much as possible while they were active, and Sara wanted to enjoy time with the family now that they were retired.

"With lists as different as these, we might as well lead separate lives," Robert said.

This wasn't the first time I'd seen couples experiencing this dilemma. After assessing their situation, I recommended a strategy that had worked with many couples in the past.

"Let's create two lists: an individual list and a couple's bucket list," I said.

I explained that the individual list would basically be identical to what each already had. The couple's list would comprise activities they both agreed they enjoyed, and none of the items would have appeared on their individual lists.

They would participate in activities on the individual list on odd numbered years. For instance, Sara has "take grandkids to Disney World" on her bucket list. On an odd numbered year, she would be free to do this. And Robert had the choice to participate or not.

On even numbered years, they would participate in activities together that appeared on the couple's list. They could also decide to complete several of the items on the lists in any one year, as long as they alternated between the couple's list and the individual list.

Sara, Robert, and I continued to meet, and as the years progressed, they expressed that the odd-even year plan using individual and couple lists was working for them. They appreciated the freedom as well as the companionship the strategy provided them.

You've invested the time and energy necessary to address the top five retirement concerns described in part 2. And by doing so, you realize why my clients have consistently expressed to me over the years that the retirement transition phase is one of the most significant experiences you'll ever go through. The good news is that over the long term, the hard work will make life easier for you and those you love. Making it this far is cause for pride and celebration!

You're now ready to explore the next stage: the Go-Go Years. This stage is go-go because it's when you're most likely your healthiest and most mobile, so you'll be go-going forward! Or maybe one of your goals is to get into shape so that your Go-Go Years are as vibrant as possible. In either case, during this stage, always focus on what you can do versus what you can't. After all, life is action, so just keep moving!

As you recall, those top five concerns discussed in part 2 came from the retirement questionnaire I sent to my clients and friends. The following is a sample of insights respondents provided me that relate to the Go-Go Years:

- Can we really afford to travel and help out the grandkids?

- Do we need to cut back on luxuries?

- How do we determine which accounts to take money from?

- Days can be long, and they need to be structured in order for me to feel my best.

- I have more time for reflection and want to spend my days with family and friends.

- Our biggest concern is maintaining our health. Our parents are both in care facilities, and we don't want to end up like them.

- I do not know how we got anything done before; we're so busy that I'm more tired now than when I was working!

- Getting involved and having a feeling of purpose can make a big difference in enjoying your retirement life.

- Never stop being passionate and never stop learning.

Do some of these comments reflect how you're feeling at this stage of your life?

Compared to the other stages, the Go-Go Years provide you the most flexibility in regard to travel plans and spending time with family and friends. Not only do you have the free time, but you also are the most physically and mentally healthy you'll be during your retirement years. So don't squander these years on the couch! Get up, explore, and create new memories.

One of my friends told me about a challenge he and others had taken concerning their own legacy. They were writing their own eulogy, and the challenge was both not to put in anything that most everyone else already knew about them and to include what they most wanted to be known for that few knew about. When I asked how he was doing with the challenge, he said it was coming along pretty well and that he was including things he had yet to do! He is in his seventies and still running several businesses!

If you've been a rule follower all your life, take risks and live outside the box. If you're not sure about participating in a particular activity, ask yourself, "Why not? What am I afraid of?" (I'm referring to risk and participation based on sound judgment and not recklessness.)

Or is it time to do something you have always wanted to do but were unable because of work? What are your passions and what would make your life better? Maybe it is time to follow your dreams and take on new challenges that will keep you in the game of life.

FEARS OVER MONEY

During the Go-Go Years, one of the biggest concerns is running out of money. There are three primary reasons why this anxiety arises. First, retirement may turn out to be more expensive than you had anticipated. Second, you may find you're in great health and anticipate living longer than you had projected. Third, the income from your retirement investments may be lower than the amounts retirement calculators previously projected.

While retirement calculators are powerful tools, they rely on historical data of various sectors that many times are back tested. This means the calculators may use current types of investments previously not available. They base past performance upon calculations related to the new investment's historical data and not the actual performance of that particular investment. In addition, the current yields on US government notes and bonds as well as corporate stocks and bonds are all below the historical norms. The bottom line of these complex issues is that it may require more assets to generate the same amount of income than was previously necessary. This, combined with longer life spans, has raised real concerns about today's retirees outlasting their money.

So what can you do to maintain as much of your financial and physical independence during the Go-Go Years?

Unfortunately, no set formula exists. In most cases, living well during your Go-Go Years requires factoring the following into your retirement plan reality:

- Keeping spending under control and preserving assets for the long term. Initially, your goal should be to preserve and grow investment assets to keep pace with inflation.

- Maintaining health, which includes regular medical physicals and being as active as you can. The more you move your body, the better your physical condition, which can help you live longer and healthier during your retirement years. Even short walks count.

- Exploring new hobbies that will bring joy and physical and mental stimulation into your life. Think about what you've always wanted to do but weren't able to because of your professional commitments.

- Having a passion for life, continuing to learn and grow, and participating in activities. These will give you purpose and can dramatically improve your Go-Go Years. Never stop learning!

- Hanging out with people who are happy and fun to be with and having humor in your life. These are great ways to extend your lifeline.

Retirement life is about finding the right balance for you!

DEVELOPING A DISTRIBUTION RETIREMENT PLAN TO SUPPORT YOU DURING YOUR GO–GO YEARS

Contrary to popular belief, the key to developing a solid distribution plan is not to focus on receiving the maximum return on your investments. Rather, it is to maximize the amount of income from those investments on a net after-tax basis.

During the Go-Go Years, you must keep in mind that taking large investment risk can be hazardous to your financial and literally to your physical health—imagine running out of money when a serious medical issue arises. Taking a big risk may leave you without the recovery time necessary to rebuild from a major loss in your investment portfolios.

By avoiding taking on large investment risk, you may still maintain income despite falling markets. But the flip side is true too; you may not see the high returns you observe when markets are rising. While my clients never complain about outperforming returns during a down market, when their returns aren't as high as what they see in a hot market, my phone will inevitably ring. The problem stems from our recency bias, which is a predisposition to allow our current perspective to be influenced more by recent events than by previous ones. This bias interferes with our ability to maintain objectivity when dealing with our own money.

If you wish to invest aggressively, then do so with an amount that will not be harmful if the investment goes south. In addition, unless you'll receive a significant inheritance, remember you're no longer adding to your investments. In a downturn, you're drawing from investments that are already decreasing in value, which erodes their value even faster.

A proper distribution retirement plan will allow you to minimize taxes and maximize income without jeopardizing your long-term financial wellness. The following steps are necessary to gain the understanding of how best to develop a distribution plan.

EVALUATING YOUR CURRENT FINANCIAL STATUS INCLUDING ASSETS AND LIABILITIES

Having a firm grasp on your current financial status is the first step to gaining control of your finances. You do this by identifying the amounts in your retirement accounts (pre-tax), personal investment accounts (after-tax), and the non-income producing assets, along with measuring the impact of carrying debt. Once you've figured out these amounts, you identify the following:

- The amount of income that will be paid from all your retirement accounts, such as pensions, annuity payments, Social Security, and deferred compensation. These accounts do not have a current liquid value but provide income over an extended period.

- The balances in all your retirement accounts that can generate income and have current known values that may be accessed. The most common examples of these are deferred annuities, IRAs, and 401(k)s.

- The balances held in all personal investment accounts, such as individual, joint, or revocable trust investment accounts; rental real estate equity and income; and cash accounts held in banks, credit unions, or money market accounts.

- The required minimum distributions (RMDs) from retirement accounts once you reach age 70½ or an estimate of them if you are younger.

- Your current living expenses broken down to those that are recurring each month, semi-annually, or annually and those that are voluntary or optional.

- Your personal financial statement showing all assets and liabilities. It is important to keep your financial statement up to date as well as obtain your credit score and credit bureau report at least annually. Other things to note in your financial statement include reviewing your debt-to-asset ratio and the amount of investment assets (income producing) as a percentage of total assets. Regardless, of how high or low your net worth is, as a rule of thumb, your debt-to-asset ratio should be no more than 25 percent, and the investment assets as a percentage of total net worth need to be at least 50 percent, although this percentage may be lower if you have a pension.

The main difference between retirement accounts and personal investment accounts is, for the most part, retirement accounts are pretax, which means the distributions are taxed as ordinary income, and personal accounts are after-tax, which means the principal is tax-free and only the dividends, interest, or capital gains are taxable, regardless of whether they are reinvested or paid out of the accounts.

TAX PLANNING: BALANCING INCOME BETWEEN PRE-TAX AND AFTER-TAX ACCOUNTS

Let's start with the good news: Once you're retired, your unemployed status means you're no longer subject to employment taxes! This saves about 7.5 percent in overall taxes. In addition, because you're no longer contributing to a retirement plan, you'll require less gross income to net out the same amount of "take-home pay" that you had while working. Overall, most people find their income tax rates are lower in retirement. They're also able to maintain their basic standard of living without making major adjustments to their spending plan. However, in order to maintain their financial independence, their budgets may require adjustments to non-essential spending.

Once you've evaluated your current financial status, you're prepared to minimize taxes by balancing between distributions from pre-tax accounts and withdrawals from after-tax accounts.

When it comes to balancing distributions and withdrawals, many people make well-intentioned but misguided mistakes. The real goal should be to find a balance that will keep your income taxes in the lowest tax bracket possible now and in the future. While many people believe their approach is meeting this objective, their actions may actually be doing the opposite. Let's explore three common strategies and their potential downsides.

50-50 Withdrawal

First, many people believe they should generate income by taking half of the net income needed from each pre-tax and after-tax accounts in order to draw equally between their portfolios. This is a 50-50 distribution and withdrawal allocation approach, and part of its appeal is its simplicity. But the 50-50 approach may not be the best solution because it does not take into account the potential income tax liability or having unequal amounts in each type of investment.

Your pre-tax income may need to include income taxes deducted from your distributions. Otherwise, you may need to make quarterly estimated tax payments. And if you miss making the estimated tax payments you may incur IRS tax penalties and interest for underpayment of taxes come April 15.

TAX–SAVING HINT: *While most tax preparers will recommend you withhold taxes from retirement plan distributions to avoid incurring IRS penalties and possible interest, let me suggest an alternative.*

When taking distributions from your IRAs, whether RMDs or not, consider taking only the net amount needed (in other words, no tax withholding) and paying the taxes from the after-tax accounts. The taxable amount of the distribution will be less, and therefore you'll reduce the income-tax liability.

This also preserves the value of the pre-tax accounts. This strategy works best when the pre-tax account is somewhat less than the after-tax portfolio values. This often happens when someone has a pension plan and has not accumulated a significant amount in other retirement accounts.

Withdraw from After–Tax Accounts

A second common strategy people take to minimize taxes is to withdraw most of their after-tax monies first. The thinking behind this is that by withdrawing after-tax monies, your income taxes in the short term will be lower than would otherwise be the case. But this approach has two downsides. First, by depleting your after-tax accounts, you limit your long-term options in the event you need large cash amounts for emergencies or larger purchases. Next, you force yourself to rely solely upon withdrawing from your pre-tax accounts once the personal accounts are depleted. This may cause increased income taxes over the long term.

Withdraw from Pre-tax Accounts

The third common strategy is just the opposite of the previous one. Rather than withdraw all your after-tax monies first, you'll deplete your pre-tax monies first. The thinking behind this approach is that you'll have much lower taxes later in life and any balance remaining in your accounts will pass down to next generation tax-free due to a step-up in basis upon your death. But the major disadvantage of this strategy is that you may be paying much higher income taxes early and not able to benefit from tax deductions later in life, which may coincide with increased medical-care expenses.

Balance All Income Sources

If the preceding strategies carry with them long-term negative tax and cash flow consequences, what's the better approach?

Unfortunately, there's no one-size-fits-all formula because everyone has different needs. With that said, the foundation of a Real Retirement Plan is the same for everyone: You must balance income from all sources in such a way that you are able to maximize sustainable income by having a thorough understanding of your income tax and cash flow needs. Skillfully tapping into various income sources is challenging because it requires you to evaluate each different type of income source. Once you've taken this step, you then need to determine the income tax liability of your particular pre-tax and after-tax balancing strategy. Last, you must figure out how to maintain the income level you'll need for your family's long-term financial security, including the big future unknown, which is our nation's healthcare system.

For the most part, I believe it's imperative to build up after-tax accounts in order for the retiree not to be solely dependent upon taxable accounts or taxable distributions. By doing so, you'll be prepared to make withdrawals from after-tax investment accounts to supplement your other income sources and maintain reserves for unexpected expenses or emergencies. Otherwise, you'll always be driving through the tax tollbooth in order to access money.

I also recommend maintaining enough of a balance in the cash portion of your liquid portfolio to support the withdrawals for at least twelve to eighteen months, so you can ride out market storms without being forced to sell in a down market.

STRATEGY HINT: *Another consideration for those who may retire earlier is to begin taking distributions from the traditional IRAs as early as age 60, rather than deferring until age 70½. By doing so, you're spreading out the taxable income over a longer period but (presumably) at a reduced tax bracket. This especially works well when the person has not yet begun to receive Social Security or other income benefits. If someone defers until required to take distributions, there will likely be more money accumulated and higher required distribution amounts. This combination may result in higher income taxes on the distributions when added to other income sources.*

A qualified financial planner and accountant can help you gain an understanding of the income tax issues associated with your retirement income and will guide you through the maze of making the proper distributions and withdrawals from your various accounts to give you the best long-term income security. They should be able to run what-if scenarios that show the different income tax and cash flow alternatives to help you make the best choices of which types of accounts to use in your retirement distribution plan.

INVESTMENT PLANNING

After you've evaluated your current financial status and have performed tax planning, you've established the foundation for the next step: investment planning. This is where you make decisions about the portfolio allocation between different asset classes and associated risk with each type of investment.

You may also make some of your portfolio allocation selections based upon where the investment is being held: in a taxable portfolio or a pre-tax or tax-deferred account. Tax planning and investment planning, while separate topics, are also interconnected.

Some assets, such as earned income, distributions from retirement accounts, and interest, will create ordinary taxable income, while capital gains (or losses) and dividends from US corporations receive more favorable tax treatment.

Some investments may be more suitable for pre-tax accounts, while others will be best in after-tax accounts. For example, would it make sense to hold municipal bonds in an IRA? Answer: No way! They are tax-free, so they do not need to be sheltered in a pre-tax account.

If you have a high-growth asset, like an individual stock, would it be better to hold it in an IRA or taxable account? Answer: It depends! If the stock has a low dividend rate and your goal is appreciation, then having it in an after-tax portfolio may be best in order to obtain favorable capital gains tax treatment. Otherwise, all that growth may be taxed as ordinary income upon distribution from the retirement account. However, a high-yielding equity portfolio with lower volatility may be suitable for a retirement account.

(And if you weren't able to answer these two questions on your own, this is one reason among many why working with a highly qualified financial adviser will benefit you.)

INVESTMENT HINT: *Hold most high-appreciation (risky) assets in after-tax accounts and most conservative assets in pre-tax accounts. The benefit of this approach is if you hold high-growth assets in an IRA and the assets take a big hit, the loss is just that: a loss! While you can write off losses in an after-tax portfolio, this isn't the case for IRAs. In other words, taking the highest risk should always be done in an after-tax account so Uncle Sam will offset some of the loss via the tax deduction if the investment does not pan out as expected.*

WITHDRAWAL RATES

When withdrawing from your investment accounts, you must always consider the amount of withdrawals compared to the overall value of the accounts. This is called a "withdrawal rate," and it can be a critical amount, especially early in your retirement years.

Just as compound returns helped you accumulate assets, the reverse is also true—if the withdrawal rate is too high, it may not be sustainable. I have simple guidelines to determine the withdrawal rate under normal life expectancy tables.

At age sixty-five, with no major health issues, consider adding another twenty years to your life expectancy. If you have had cancer, heart disease, or diabetes at or before you reached age sixty-five, then your life expectancy may be somewhat shorter than what the tables suggest.

The following is a basic guide. Keep in mind for every rule, there are exceptions. At the same time, this table should give you some sense of the amounts that can be withdrawn from investment portfolios at various ages. Note that the younger you start withdrawals, the lower the withdrawal percentage should be and that the withdrawal percentages are progressive as you age:

AGE BAND FOR DISTRIBUTIONS, PROGRESSIVE

Age	Distribution
50 to 60	3% or less
61 to 70	4% or less
71 to 75	5% or less
76 to 80	6% or less
81 to 85	8% or less
Over 85	Variable

Why is the distribution for over eighty-five years old variable? Because your withdrawal rate at this stage depends on your health and financial needs. However, this is a very general guideline, and the withdrawal rates can vary for any age. For example, many individuals have higher health-care needs earlier in their lives. As such, their withdrawal rates may be much higher at earlier ages but will most likely be for a shorter period due to reduced life expectancies.

If you're in a care facility, then the withdrawal percentages may be much higher than those for someone living independently in his or her home with no mortgage. At some point, you or your spouse may require long-term care (statistics show that one in three people will need long-term care services in their lifetime). To prepare for this possibility, you'll also need to evaluate the sustainability of paying for it when the time comes to enter a care facility. For basic independent living in a continuing care retirement community (CCRC), the cost may be less than three thousand dollars per month. But this amount can quickly escalate if more services are required. Memory care facilities tend to be the highest, with monthly costs well above ten thousand dollars. Having an LTC policy can greatly reduce the risk of spending down all your assets. This is especially important if you have a spouse and you would like to leave him or her with resources in the event of your passing.

In the past thirty years, I've had many retirees who lived into their eighties and nineties and maintained their real net spendable income ("real" means inflation adjusted) with withdrawal rates that were a bit higher than what appear in the table. At the same time, I'm cautioning against having higher withdrawal rates in the future because I believe that long-term portfolio returns of the past thirty to forty years may not be sustainable due to forthcoming changes in demographics and public policy.

There are several significant questions that the future holds:

- The baby boomers have provided a wave of prosperity for all Americans. But as they retire and pass away, will the next generations be able to maintain such a high pace of growth and expansion?

- How will technology affect the average worker?

- Will the middle class cease to exist?

- Will the US government need to provide a minimum income to all citizens in order to maintain the economy, or will new ideas and innovations require a different type of workforce?

- How long will Social Security and Medicare be financially viable? Will the government be required to reduce benefits, defer the age of eligibility, or initiate a means test (based upon income) to receive benefits?

- What amount of income taxes or employment taxes will be necessary to support the government programs if the deficit continues to grow at the current pace?

These are major discussions for another time but topics to be aware of in coming years.

TIMING OF SOCIAL SECURITY AND DISTRIBUTIONS FROM IRAS AND OTHER INCOME–PRODUCING ASSETS

I often tell my clients, "If you would only give me your date of death, planning would be much easier!" No doubt, the timing of Social Security and distributions is one of the most important and difficult decisions you'll make during the Go-Go Years. Proper timing is a critical step to maximize income and minimize taxes. You have multiple variables to consider, and the impact of your decisions will have long-term consequences.

In some situations, you may benefit from withdrawing from IRA accounts before reaching age 70½. This is often the case under several situations: when deferring the start of Social Security, when retiring prior to becoming eligible for full Social Security benefits, or when personal investment accounts are relatively small compared to your pre-tax accounts.

The distribution or withdrawal amount taken at an early age may only be an amount needed to meet your current cash flow needs, and it may not be your RMD amount. Once you have reached age 59½, you can make withdrawals from IRA accounts without a penalty. There is no required withdrawal minimum or a maximum between ages 59½ and 70½. You must weigh this information against the benefit of deferring Social Security or needing income if you have retired earlier.

Another option for those who can afford to retire in their forties or fifties is taking what is referred to as the "72(t) election." The "72(t)" refers to the actual IRS tax code. Under this election plan, you can begin withdrawing from your IRA before age 59½ if the amounts are based on your life expectancy and the distributions are the same every month until you reach 59½.

You take your life expectancy and then divide the value of the account by the number of years. For example, a fifty-year-old man has a life expectancy of thirty years. If the value of his IRA is $500,000, then he would calculate his annual distribution by dividing $500,000 by 30, which is $16,666 per year.

There are situations where deferring RMDs and/or Social Security may not be the best choice. In these situations, people may not have saved substantial amounts in either after-tax accounts or pre-tax accounts, so they become dependent upon taking Social Security at full retirement age (FRA), which is age sixty-six for anyone born before 1955 and then gradually rises to age sixty-seven for those born between 1955 and 1960. Or in other situations, a widow may begin taking Social Security at age sixty, and a divorced spouse may be eligible as early as age sixty-two.

There are many other reasons for starting Social Security early or taking distributions from retirement accounts. Family medical expenses or unemployment or disability can all trigger the need to begin benefits early.

SOCIAL SECURITY NOTE: *My belief is that the government will need to raise the FRA to age seventy in the not-so distant future as a way to maintain Social Security retirement benefits for most of retirees. In addition, it may need to implement a phase-out of benefits for those with incomes over specified amounts. In other words, the one percenters may not qualify in the future.*

In 2015, the government made big changes to Social Security. The Social Security Administration placed a new restriction on taking advantage of benefits between spouses. Previously, under "file and suspend," an eligible spouse (called the primary beneficiary) could file for Social Security benefits and his or her partner could also apply for spousal benefits. Immediately afterwards, eligible spouses could suspend their benefits and defer them until a later age in order to obtain a higher benefit. Meanwhile, the spouse receiving spousal benefits could also defer the start of benefits based upon his or her contribution record to obtain a higher benefit at a later age, which is usually seventy years old.

In this way, one spouse could receive income from spousal benefits, and both could defer up to age seventy to obtain the maximum benefits from Social Security based upon his or her earning records.

The government decided this was allowing Social Security beneficiaries to take advantage of the system. Therefore, Uncle Sam closed this loophole by no longer allowing the "file and suspend" option. The new restriction was implemented at the end of 2015 with an exception for anyone who turned age sixty-two prior to January 1, 2016.

So, what happens to the rest of us? After April 2016, the new provisions required that the primary beneficiaries receiving Social Security had to continue receiving benefits in order for their spouses to obtain benefits. Going forward, you'll not be able to benefit from electing spousal benefits and letting your own benefit grow until age seventy. You will need to take the benefit at FRA, or you may defer to a later age up to age seventy, but not obtain both spousal and individual benefits in the future.

This creates a planning opportunity for couples where the partner wanting to take spousal benefits was born before January 1, 1954. If one spouse is currently receiving Social Security benefits and the partner turns age sixty-six, then that partner can obtain spousal benefits and defer his or her Social Security until age seventy. If you are in this group, don't forget to take advantage of this option!

LIVING ALTERNATIVES

During your Go-Go Years, you have many options regarding where you'll live as the years progress. You also have the time to commit to determining the types of care you may need as your abilities change. From aging in place to nursing home care, in the following section, we'll explore some of the choices you have.

Aging in Place

According to my experience, most people want to remain living independently for as long as possible. Many seek to live out their lives in the place they call home—whether they've lived there for decades or only a few years—and don't want to be in a planned community. This scenario describes "aging in place."

I recall how, when the topic of moving as a consequence of aging came up, my mother-in-law would always say she needed to clean the closets before she would consider selling the house. She maintained that line for five years. Unfortunately, by the time she could no longer take care of herself and had to leave her home for good, my wife and I wound up overseeing her move, which included cleaning the closets.

There's nothing wrong with wanting to age in place. But if you decide to do so, you want to make sure you're living in a community that has resources to provide the assistance you'll need when you're less mobile and that you have access to good medical care when things don't go as planned. You also must consider your ability to navigate your home as your body changes as you age.

Does your house have stairs that you'll eventually struggle to climb? Will you be able to enter and exit the home easily? Will you need to build a different entrance, and will doors be wide enough to allow for a wheelchair? Will you need to convert a tub into a shower and install railings so you can safely shower?

You may be able to modify your home, so you can safely live in it over the long term, or you may realize aging in place is hazardous to your safety and health if not now but in the future.

Oftentimes, when you're in the position of having to decide about aging in place, you may find it difficult to consider the consequences of doing so. For example, one reason people seek to age in place is to remain close to friends. While this is perfectly legitimate, when you decide this, you also want to consider if this choice comes at the exclusion of your family.

The harsh reality is that friends move away (sometimes to be closer to their own families), friends will most likely not take care of you, and they pass away. If you age in place to be close to friends and this decision leaves you far from family, pretty soon you could find yourself isolated, which creates a whole series of problems from difficulty accessing medical care when you need it to depression and anxiety. Keep in mind that being alone may result in a lack of interaction with others, and this can also contribute to dementia.

With that said, if you're in an area with resources for both homecare and medical care and family or friends or both are reasonably close by, aging in place over the long term may work out well for you.

I had a client that had no family. When she retired, she was living independently in her condominium and enjoying life. Unfortunately, she was diagnosed with cancer two years later and required increasing medical care. Despite her age and cancer, she was determined to age in place. Together, she and I planned how to manage her care. She had resources in her community that would allow her to age in place. As a result, she was able to remain in her home for the next two and half years. The last three weeks of her life, she spent in hospice care. Up to the last six months of her life, she remained active and appreciated that she was able to maintain as much independence as possible.

Aging in place skillfully requires having an honest conversation with your family (if applicable) or friends or both. It also requires developing a strategy that will provide your needed care and forming a team of professionals who can fulfill a managed care plan.

You must develop a plan that can be implemented in the event of a change in circumstances in which you may need assistance for a shorter or longer period than you had anticipated. For example, imagine you broke a leg or hip. Suddenly, your mobility has become an issue. Who will go shopping for you, prepare your meals, and help you get up in the morning and get dressed—not to mention bathe and use the toilet? These are not always the most fun topics to think about, but if you fail to address these issues, then you're delegating these tasks to someone else.

Senior–Only or Adult–Only Communities

For those who may be looking for a place to enjoy their Go-Go Years, this option may be for you. Note that these are the only types of housing that can be discriminatory; these communities can reject your application based on your age, and children aren't allowed to live in these communities. The main advantages of senior- or adult-only communities are the residences themselves are low maintenance, provide a secure environment, and may have convenient services such as restaurants and transportation to recreation, entertainment, and medical facilities. In addition, many offer a wide variety of activities from golf and tennis to swimming, biking, horseback riding, and boating.

While in most adult living communities, the residents tend to be in their Go-Go Years, some may be connected to continuing care retirement communities (which you'll read about in the next section), or residents may need to move once again when they enter the Slow-Go or No-Go Years.

The primary disadvantages are that there may be a high cost to entry, and you may need to move to obtain assisted care services in the future.

NOTE: *It is critical to understand what amount of buy-in is necessary and whether you will receive a partial or full refund upon leaving. In some cases, you own your new home or condo and are responsible for selling it once you leave. In other situations, the adult communities do not provide any assisted living services in the event you need them, but you can obtain services from outside organizations nearby. In order to avoid surprise and skyrocketing costs, you must take these factors into account when evaluating your decisions to relocate into a senior-only or adult-only community.*

Continuing Care Retirement Communities (CCRCs)

CCRCs are designed to allow as much independence as possible for their residents while providing care options in the event an acute need arises or one's health changes. In many instances, however, the residents are still driving and able to manage their own care.

When needed, most will provide in-home care within certain limits and access to nursing staff. If you have a need for more intensive care, then you may end up staying in a rehab facility, which is a temporary facility, to recover from surgery or illness, or you may need to move to an assisted care facility if longer-term care is required. If circumstances warrant, CCRCs may offer nursing home and memory care options as well. These types of communities are the most comprehensive because they provide the widest range of services among different care facilities.

Some of my clients have bought into golf-based CCRCs that include a large single-family home with views of the green. In the event they require assisted care, services are available on site. Other clients have purchased a condominium in a CCRC that they own and will pass down to their heirs. I've also had clients who have paid an initial fee to enter the CCRC and have refund options upon relocating or death.

TAX HINT: *All CCRCs and other medical assistance facilities require monthly payments for basic services. Portions of these are tax deductible as medical expenses. Most facilities provide an annual statement reflecting the tax-deductible costs or percentage of cost attributable to medical care. If you require more services, then the tax deduction amount will go up because the increased services are usually connected to the amount of healthcare you need.*

THREE WHAT-IF SCENARIOS DURING THE GO-GO YEARS

What if my spouse dies before me?

Working with a financial advisor, George and Connie did a remarkable job planning for their future. Connie was sixty-six years old and had decided to wait until she turned seventy years old to receive her Social Security and RMDs. George was a few years older and had a US government pension after almost forty years of public service. They had paid off their mortgage and were living well within their means.

Together they made a list of the places they wanted to visit and things that they wanted to do in their retirement years. The couple definitely planned well in order to maintain their financial wellbeing throughout their retired years.

Two years after they retired, George died of a heart attack at age seventy. His sudden passing left him falling far short of what they'd anticipated based on following the life expectancy table. As the saying goes, "Life holds no guarantees." At the same time, statistically speaking, women are most likely to be single at some point in their retirement lives. Connie just didn't expect that time to come so soon.

The impact of George's unexpected death brought everything to a standstill for Connie. She was fortunate that she had the resources; George had retained his life insurance with a death benefit of five hundred thousand dollars, and she was the beneficiary of his pension.

George's Social Security benefits terminated upon his death. But Connie had the option of receiving, as a survivor benefit, the amount he had been earning. She could then switch to her own benefit, if higher, upon her turning age seventy. Their assets were either jointly held or listed the other as the beneficiary. As such, there were no probate issues because all George's assets were transferred directly to Connie. This eliminated probate and allowed her to retain the assets necessary to maintain her long-term financial wellness.

Financially, Connie was going to be in good shape. But emotionally, she struggled. At sixty-eight years old, she was now single, and all their retirement travel plans were suddenly useless. She would be able to recover over time with the help of family, friends, and her faith. She was committed to overcome George's death and maintain her independence. The planning they had put in place ahead of time made all the difference for her to be able to focus on dealing with her loss and working through her emotions.

Although not an issue in Connie's case, another matter can arise when a spouse passes at any time during retirement: the impact the death has on the children. Often, this is not recognized immediately. I recall one case where the father died leaving his wife of fifty-five years, two adult children, and five grandchildren. They were a couple of faith and had a close relationship with their church pastor. To his credit, the man of the cloth spent a significant amount of time consoling the wife. Unfortunately, he did not invest any time helping the adult children and grandchildren deal with their loss.

Many times, the children want to step in and try to help the surviving elder parent, regardless of whether that mother or father wants the help. The discussion the children generally have is what to do with Mom now that Dad has passed away (or vice versa). The following are common and, often important, questions:

- Should the surviving parent stay in the current residence, move closer to one of the children, or even consider moving in with one of the children?

- Who is going to manage the surviving parent's finances?

- What if the surviving parent is no longer able to drive? How will he or she buy food or visit the doctor's office?

- Who is going to look after the surviving parent and be responsible for his or her wellbeing?

- Which child is the successor trustee or executor?

Most times, the children think they will all be the co-trustees, regardless of how many there are. They then are surprised that only one child has been named. That may cause more discussions and many times creates animosity among siblings. These conflicts could be easily avoided if the parents included the children ahead of time in a family meeting, where the parents would discuss their intentions concerning their estate.

I have found if the surviving parent is able to continue living independently and is reasonably healthy and mobile, then he or she generally prefers to stay in his or her own environment, especially if the parent has been in the house for an extended period and has many friends in the area. My suggestion for adult children is to have the "where do you want to live?" and "who is going to take care of you?" discussions with the surviving parent before the funeral of the deceased parent, not after. In fact, I recommend you have the discussion before anything happens to either of them. For example, you can ask both or either parent, "What would you want to do about where to live when one of you passes away?"

You will find that a parent's desire to remain in his or her environment can trump common sense in making good decisions, especially in the near term. Even if Mom has not been driving for some period and reliable transportation resources in her area aren't easily accessible, she may still not want to make a major move shortly after the death of her spouse. A surviving parent's judgment all depends upon his or her emotional state and what he or she may have planned before the partner's death.

Another issue arises when the surviving parent is in need of care or is already in a retirement facility. Will the children want him or her to move closer to them, or will they want to move closer to the parent? The impact of these decisions can be dramatic from many points of view. From adult children's employment and the children's own retirement plans being put on hold to the impact upon the grandchildren, relocating either a parent or the adult children (and their own families if applicable) can create many issues.

If you're caring for a parent and have a son or daughter needing your attention, you may feel torn between meeting the needs of both if their needs conflict. For instance, do you live closer to one versus the other? Do you have any financial responsibility to take care of either? What about your spouse? How will these decisions impact your relationship with him or her?

My experience working with clients has taught me that making these difficult decisions takes time. If you're the parent, having these tough conversations with your children about your future will greatly reduce the potential for family conflict. If you do not confront these issues ahead of time, you're leaving them for someone else, such as children, other relatives, or professionals, to decide for you. To avoid this predicament, make sure you have a solid estate plan and you have communicated its contents to your family members that will be impacted by you or your spouse's passing. Doing so will help the transition after the death of a spouse and avoid the conflicts that typically arise among the children trying to help during this emotionally charged period.

I also recommend parents leave a letter of instruction as to their wishes for funeral arrangements and any particular possessions that they want left to specific individuals.

What if I'm single at retirement?

Eileen had been married but divorced when she was in her mid-forties and had a son. At the time of the break-up, her son was fifteen years old, and her parents were living about four hours away.

Ten years later, her dad passed away, and her son moved to the West Coast to take a new job at a high-tech company. Eileen's elderly mom was able to maintain her independence; she lived modestly in a rural area in a mortgage-free, small house.

However, when Eileen was about sixty and thinking of her retirement, her mother was diagnosed with Alzheimer's disease. Eileen had a brother, but he did not live in the area and was eking by, so he was unable to help personally or financially.

This meant that Eileen became the sole caregiver. She put her life on hold, helped obtain the assistance her mother needed, and took over the management of her mom's healthcare and finances. Eventually,

Eileen realized her mother could no longer live on her own and needed to move into Eileen's house to be close by. After the move, Eileen put her mom's house on the market; it took nearly a year to sell.

During the day, when Eileen worked, she had daytime caregivers. At night, her mom was all hers. Eileen was very concerned that her mother, who was physically healthy, might outlive her resources. Eileen decided to postpone her own retirement. When Eileen was sixty-five, her mother needed more care than Eileen could provide, so she moved her into a memory care facility that dramatically increased her monthly bills. Her mother was now drawing down her resources even with the house being sold. Eileen calculated that her mom would run out of money in about three years.

During that period, Eileen never had me time. Her life was put on hold because she worked each day and took full responsibility for her mother's care when she arrived home. Two years later, her mom passed away, and Eileen felt she could finally retire. Afterwards, she began to feel she could think about herself; she had a newfound freedom. She could now work in her garden or go meet friends on a Wednesday and crack crabs together in Annapolis.

Many retirees are finding their Go-Go Years may be impacted by having parents still living and needing help with a variety of issues, from managing their bills to obtaining the support they require to help them move to a care facility. My recommendation is, as much as possible, to avoid going it alone because being a caregiver can become an exhausting task. Seek help and remind yourself that you're entitled to have a fulfilling retirement life too!

What if I receive an inheritance?

Several years into Patrick and Frances's retirement, Patrick's wealthy uncle died. Throughout his life, Uncle Brian was very close to Patrick. He had no kids, and in his advanced years, Patrick and Frances took care of him as if he were their own parent. He had a significant estate and left a good deal to charity but made a specific bequest to Patrick and Frances of five hundred thousand dollars and to their two adult children of one hundred thousand dollars each.

Although Patrick didn't win the lottery, the income came in very handy because the couple felt freer about their own retirement plans. In addition, their children would have resources to help them and their own families without having to depend upon Patrick and Frances for financial help.

Upon further reflection, the couple decided this extra money could provide them a new opportunity; they planned to leave a small financial legacy to their grandchildren by funding college savings accounts and adding a direct benefit to the grandchildren from their estate. As a result, they revised their estate plan by amending their family revocable trust in order to reflect their intentions for their grandchildren.

LIVING WELL DURING YOUR GO-GO YEARS

During the Go-Go Years, most of us want to be as physically and mentally active as possible. By establishing a plan that addresses your available cash flow and living within your means, you have done your part to build a secure retirement foundation that will allow you to really enjoy this stage over the long term.

If you're looking for a place to start your search for financial guidance, I recommend working with a Certified Financial Planner professional. CFPs have been trained to help people like you make the most of their retirement lives. Visit the Financial Planning Association website at www.fpanet.org or the CFP website at www.LetsMakeaPlan.org or www.CFP.org to find a CFP in your area.

What's right for you? Each situation is different, and the answer to this question always starts with "it depends!" A reputable financial adviser can help you navigate your retirement skillfully. He or she will focus on maximizing income and minimizing income taxes while preserving and growing your overall assets in order to provide your desired long-term financial security.

CHAPTER 11

SLOW-GO YEARS

Life happens while we are making other plans.

– John Lennon

"**L**ATELY, IT SEEMS LIKE I'm spending more time at the doctor's office than anywhere else," said Sally.

The retiree was on the phone with her daughter, Jennifer, complaining about the changes she had experienced in recent years.

"And then you should see my medicine cabinet! So many prescription bottles, you'd think it was an ER crash cart," she said.

Sally thought about how long it took every week to fill her Monday-through-Sunday pillbox. Prior to retiring, she had no idea how many meds she'd have to take.

Jennifer worried about the ramifications of her mom's complaints. Was the uptick in doctor's visits and prescription medications a sign her mom would soon need to make major decisions about her future?

Jennifer's concerns were legitimate. Her mother's deteriorating health would mostly likely require her to make important quality-of-life decisions in the near term. This signaled Sally's transition into the Slow-Go Years, a stage usually characterized by significant changes in your living arrangements.

MULTIPLE FACTORS INFLUENCE WHERE TO LIVE DURING YOUR SLOW-GO YEARS

"I am starting to think I will never be old enough to know better."

As Sally's example points out, one of the major considerations that will influence where you'll live is your health. Maybe you or your spouse has experienced health changes that have resulted in less mobility. Or maybe your spouse's health scare was so severe you had to face the prospect of being a widow or widower. As a result, you may have realized it's time to think harder than ever about transitioning into a retirement-living community or relocating to be closer to family or friends. These are both common choices.

The following is a sample of insights survey respondents provided me that relate to the Slow-Go Years:

- I retired early and continued to work part time until I was seventy-six. My wife continued to work for a number of years after my retirement. This allowed us to have more financial security, and now we're looking at downsizing and moving near our children and grandchildren.

- My kids are suggesting I move closer to them or into a retirement living community that offers independent living as well as various levels of care.

- I hate the thought of moving or going to an assisted care facility.

- I didn't expect to have to make so many changes to my home in order to accommodate my reduced mobility.

- The older I get, the harder I find it to make changes.

- Maybe I'll die before having to make a move!

- Trying to find a place is depressing. I cannot find anywhere I look forward to moving to.

- Think about what you can do, not what you can't do!

- As you age, you don't lose interest in sex, but you lose your power!

Last, the following response came from one of my dear clients that lived in the same house for over fifty years. She had one child and two grandchildren that lived nearby. Over the years, her house became more of a burden as her physical health declined. She struggled navigating the home's narrow hallways and stairs. She also found it more physically challenging to make doctors' appointments in order to receive the help she needed. During the day, she spent most of her time alone, reading and watching TV. She said:

> Moving to the retirement community was one of the best decisions I've ever made. I didn't realize just how lonely I was. Prior to moving, I had family close, but now I see I craved interacting with others my age. I got involved in several committees and have a new spunk in my walk! I even had my own "wake party" last year. I figured that I shouldn't miss out on the fun and wanted to know what might be said about me!

Does anything you've read from these retirees reflect how you're feeling at this stage of your life?

The Slow-Go Years don't mean you're stranded in your house or retirement facility all day and unable to get around.

In fact, you probably know or have at least heard of men and women who are playing golf into their eighties and nineties . . . and I'm not referring to golf scores here. Their pace is a bit slower than what it used to be, and what took a nine iron to reach the green now requires a seven or even a five iron. Regardless of the reduced pace, the inspiring part is they are still having a good time with their friends.

In my case, I play with a gentleman who is eighty-three years old, and he generally beats me. This frustrates me to no end. He loves seeing the expression on my face after his drive goes about 125 to 150 yards, then proceeds to hit each of his next shots down the middle and onto the green, and at the end, one putts! I'm a bogey player, which means I score in the nineties. Meanwhile, he generally scores in the high eighties or low nineties.

Another couple I know are both over ninety and go out in the evening to play the first two holes at our club. The first hole takes them out, and the second hole brings them back close to the clubhouse. It takes them about forty-five minutes to play the two holes. But they couldn't care less about how much time they require because they're enjoying the moment! As these examples point out, the Slow-Go Years usually mean you're not able to do as much as you have in the past. At the same time, you can still participate in many normal activities, just at a reduced pace.

THE UPSIDE TO DOWNSIZING

This stage of life is when you may want to make those difficult decisions about downsizing, which usually means relocating in this context. Many clients have expressed that downsizing sounds negative, as if it's something you're forced to do, rather than a choice. I'll use relocating instead. Relocating often requires decluttering your home and eliminating many of the possessions you've accumulated over your lifetime. Unfortunately, too many in the Slow-Go Years interpret relocating as the beginning of the end. And this often leads to putting off taking important action. But rather than the end of life as you know it, it's actually the beginning of a new stage that will provide you as much freedom and independence as possible. By playing center stage in your own life, *you* are taking control of your future, and you're not leaving it to someone else.

Have you made plans to finance the cost of long-term care, and have you purchased LTC policies? If so, make sure you've written your intentions down, and be sure you've identified other income sources. For example, you can generate additional money through selling your home, obtaining a reverse mortgage, selling your life insurance policy, withdrawing cash value from whole life policies, dipping into retirement accounts and personal investments, and selling personal property such as a car that is no longer needed or old jewelry that the children do not want. Just remember that furniture, unless an antique, has little value other than the amount you'll receive by donating it.

You can speed up the decluttering process by including your family members. For instance, you can give your adult children a chance to provide input regarding what items they want for themselves.

Remember that each child has had a different life experience with his or her parents. Children's memories can vary dramatically from one sibling to the next. When involving your children in the decluttering process, consider asking them to provide you a list of items they would most like to keep upon your passing. Or you can take the opposite approach: Provide a list of items that you've designated specific children will receive. You can include this list with your estate documents. Most of the time, your executor or successor trustee will be charged to carry out your wishes upon your passing, and having a letter of instruction from you can make that job much easier.

Many people I know who have made the relocating decision were really happy they did once the headache of moving was behind them and they had eliminated much of the "stuff" via gifting to family, friends, and charitable organizations. With a big burden lifted off their shoulders, they felt less anxiety and more freedom.

After removing their excess stuff, some moved into retirement communities, continuing care retirement communities, or simply a smaller, more manageable home or condo in their local community. If they stayed close to the house they left, they were able to maintain their friendships while also feeling freer to "lock and leave" on a vacation without worrying about if a tree fell on the house while they were away.

Others have downsized and moved farther away from their homes and into a smaller one that is in a completely new location. Sometimes they did this to be closer to family. Other times, it was to live in a warmer climate or in an area with a lower cost of living or both. Those who have done this well have made the decision early in their retirement planning. By doing so, they gave themselves time to establish new friendships and take more control over their environment during a time when they were as physically and mentally healthy as possible. In some cases, people purchased a second home before retiring with the intention of relocating to it once they retired. Prior to retirement, it was a vacation home, where they spent their holidays preparing it for their permanent move. By the time it came to relocate, they had already taken care of most of the hard work. As a result, the move went smoothly.

One's environment can be a major stumbling block for many who wait too long to make a moving decision. As we age, the job of going through all the possessions we've accumulated over a lifetime can be daunting. I've also observed that possessions often take on more importance as people age because during this stage of life retirees crave security and being surrounded by our belongings makes them feel safer. Also, during this stage, adjusting to changes in your surroundings becomes more difficult (we're creatures of habit, after all), as does getting rid of all the stuff that has been accumulated—just the mere thought of decreasing your belongings can stress you out and push you into procrastination.

Delaying taking action because they claim "I'll know when it's time" is sadly the reason why many people wait too long and then have no choice in arranging where to live and what kind of care they'll receive. The truth is there's no time like the present. If you convince yourself otherwise, you'll always find a reason to postpone taking action.

I've found that it's also harder to make critical relocating decisions as we age. People experiencing dementia struggle making simple decisions, let alone complex, big ones. For example, given three or more clothing choices, those with dementia often find themselves suffering from information overload, which leads to confusion and indecision. Or a restaurant menu, full of options, may lead to similar bewilderment. People at this stage of life are clearly ill-equipped to make major healthcare and relocation decisions. (As an aside, in the restaurant and clothing scenarios, limiting choices leads to more clarity and less uncertainty on the part of those with some form of dementia.)

In the next section, we'll explore the pitfalls that exist in your Slow-Go Years through the experiences of a couple, Max and Elizabeth.

RELOCATING DONE RIGHT

Max and Elizabeth were in their late sixties. Max had suffered a heart attack the year before. Fortunately, he had made a full recovery. But the scare motivated the couple to downsize and move into a retirement community while they were both relatively healthy and could do so on their own terms.

During their transition into retirement stage, the couple had developed a Real Retirement Plan. As a result, they were prepared to make tough decisions while maintaining an objective perspective. Researching care facilities was one of the steps they had taken during this stage. After they found one they liked, they submitted a deposit, which put them at the top of the move-in list when the time came to enter it.

Initially, Max and Elizabeth imagined relocating would be a straightforward process: identifying the things they wanted to keep and then getting rid of the rest of the stuff that they no longer needed. Once they started, however, they quickly understood how much effort reducing the clutter would take. They'd lived in the house for decades. Every room and closet was filled and now needed to be emptied. From clothes and furniture to appliances, most of these belongings hadn't been used in years.

In the midst of the relocating chaos, Max and Elizabeth's daughter found them a real estate agent who had developed a niche helping retirees downsize. The agent worked with a company that specialized in elder moves. The agent and her team helped the couple determine what to discard, donate, sell, gift to family, and, last, bring with them to their new home.

A process they initially thought would take a few weeks, maximum, required a whopping six months. As much as it was a struggle to liquidate their house, they knew they could have never done it as efficiently and effectively without professional help. Paying their team was worth every penny and reminded them of when they worked with a wedding planner when their daughter married. They experienced a similar level of satisfaction this time, as they did when they hired the wedding planner years ago. In the end, they were glad they took charge of the process when they were able-bodied, rather than waiting and then having to delegate major decisions to someone who probably wouldn't have fulfilled all their wishes.

With the relocating behind them, Max and Elizabeth moved into the retirement community they had chosen, one that was nearby their children and grandchildren. They hadn't brought much with them, but the small collection of family heirlooms and photos held significant emotional value to the couple. Once in their retirement community, they quickly made friends and participated in many of its activities. Their family members came to visit often, and Max and Elizabeth frequently went to their children's houses as well.

A couple of years later, Elizabeth came down with pneumonia, and the illness took her life a few months later. Their LTC policy covered her expenses during the last six months of her life. For two years after her passing, Max continued to live as independently as he had when Elizabeth was with him. He then began having memory lapses that resulted in dementia. When he could no longer take care of himself, he was moved into an assisted care facility within the community itself. The couple's LTC policy covered the majority of his expenses once he entered the assisted care facility. Thanks to their LTC insurance, they were able to maintain financial independence and the best case for living well during the Slow-Go Years. With the LTC insurance, they were able to leave a financial legacy to their children and grandchildren.

CARE OPTIONS:
ASSISTED-LIVING FACILITIES AND FAMILY CAREGIVERS

When aging in place will no longer allow you to live as well as possible during your Slow-Go Years, you must adapt to change, which means broadening your options and moving into an assisted-living facility. These facilities provide services such as laundry, housekeeping, meals, and twenty-four-hour monitoring. Usually, residents can take care of their own personal care and basic needs. Assisted care facilities may have rehab services for use on a temporary basis, and in many instances, people move to assisted care facilities after living in senior-only or adult-only communities, which may not have offered any care options.

Assisted living facilities are generally offered within a continuing care retirement community, while there are also assisted care options run as independent, stand-alone facilities. In either case, the cost for assisted living services can vary widely. Often, they charge a base monthly fee; from there, you'll pay additional amounts depending on the level of services you need. If you need a memory care unit for dementia, the cost can jump significantly. This is because providing those with dementia a safe environment and access to medical staff is a round-the-clock endeavor and requires a more professional staff that has a higher level of training.

The main advantage of assisted care facilities is that you have ongoing care being provided, and it usually includes meals, medication oversight, access to doctors, and transportation. The disadvantage is rooted in one's emotions. Moving to an assisted care facility may be a psychological blow that signals giving up your independence and may seem the equivalent of a nursing home, which feels like incapacity or death or both are near.

For generations, family members have been the most common type of caregiver during one's Slow-Go Years. Before the onset of many of the preceding options, family caregivers were the only choice besides nursing homes; they were typically the spouses and daughters of those requiring care. This is still sometimes the case. But when adult children are charged with taking on the duties of family caregiver, this may put them in a difficult position if they live far away or have their own nuclear family commitments or both.

The main advantages of this option are the low costs to the recipients and the high degree of comfort and trust they have in their caregivers (this isn't always the case, though). The main disadvantage is if the spouse is the primary caregiver, he or she may not have the ability to meet the needs of the wife or husband. And if providing care is overly taxing, this may deteriorate the caregiver's own health.

WHAT IF I DON'T WANT MY ESTATE TO GO TO MY CHILD'S SPOUSE?

Rob and Ryann love their daughter, Ann, unconditionally. But they aren't big fans of her husband, Bruce. Their son-in-law has a history of making terrible financial decisions, including squandering his and Ann's money on a get-rich-quick scheme that would have left them bankrupt had it not been for Rob and Ryann bailing them out.

Upon their passing, Rob and Ryann wanted nothing more than to leave their estate to their daughter. But it was Ann's husband they were worried about. They knew if Bruce had access to the money they left for Ann, his terrible financial decisions could leave the couple broke once again.

When the couple entered their Slow-Go Years, they spent time reevaluating their estate plan. Rob and Ryann wanted to figure out a way to support their daughter while decreasing the risk of her husband's poor financial judgment to their legacy. Doing so would require the services of an elder law attorney. They hired the lawyer who recommended setting up a family trust so that it would provide the desired income to their daughter during her lifetime but excluded the son-in-law from having any access to the funds held by the trust.

The lawyer drafted the family trust so that a professional trustee was employed as the successor, and in that way, Ann would not be blamed for refusing to distribute monies to her husband. If Ann predeceased her husband, the monies would solely be used for the benefit of Ann's children (the grandchildren of Rob and Ryann). This is sometimes referred to as a generation-skipping trust (GST).

This type of estate planning can also work well when there is a child or in-law that has other bad habits such as drug or alcohol abuse. In all such cases, an elder law or estate tax attorney needs to be consulted to find the best solution for your particular needs.

LIVING WELL DURING YOUR SLOW-GO YEARS

As Henry David Thoreau said, "Our life is frittered away by detail. Simplify, simplify." A large part of how the Slow-Go Years will provide you as much freedom and independence as possible is by simplifying your life. By taking the steps to modify your home, downsize, or relocate, you're setting yourself up to enjoy your life on your own terms and not depending upon others to make the difficult choices for you.

If aging in place is a comforting scenario for you, you're not alone. Most of us link freedom and independence with our homes. But if aging in place doesn't align with your current physical ability or your plans for the future, then maintaining the status quo may wind up leading to less, not more, freedom and independence in the future.

Along with simplifying your life, adapting to change is another fundamental quality of living well during your Slow-Go Years. After reading this chapter, you now realize that aging in place may be one step along a series of care options you'll need. By maintaining a flexible mindset, you'll navigate each transition with more ease and less stress than if you insisted on one particular option and refused to budge from your position.

Last, no single care option will correspond with all people at a certain age. What's right for you depends on your financial status, health, preferences, location, and spouse and family situation. In this chapter, I've provided you choices and described their advantages and disadvantages. Armed with this information, you're preparing yourself to live well during your Slow-Go Years.

CHAPTER 12

NO-GO YEARS

Humor and laughing keep you alive.

That and waking up every morning.

– Survey respondent

DURING MY MEETING WITH my client Natalie, she expressed her concerns about her mom's insistence on driving despite her advanced age and diminished vision and reflexes.

"She's a danger on the road to herself and others! My brother, sister, and I met with Mom to convince her to give up her car keys. But no matter how hard we tried, she wouldn't budge," Natalie said.

After the family intervention plan flopped, Natalie decided to contact her mom's oncologist. Her mother had begun undergoing breast cancer treatment six months prior and recently had a mastectomy.

During her latest appointment with her oncologist, the doctor informed her that she shouldn't drive any more.

"My mom called me right after her appointment," Natalie told me. She said, "I didn't know getting my breast removed meant I couldn't drive anymore.'"

COMMON CHANGES IN THE NO-GO YEARS

When you've been in the financial services industry as long as I have, you're given an intimate look into people's lives over the long term. I won't paint a brighter picture than what reality has revealed to me about the No-Go Years. They are often some of the most difficult my clients have experienced and for their families as well. This is mainly because of the decrease in physical or cognitive ability or both. This stage marks a significant departure from the previous ones because the No-Go Years mean that you are most likely no longer in control of your circumstances, and this limits your ability to make independent decisions.

As far as physical abilities are concerned, during the No-Go Years, your hearing and vision may have deteriorated significantly from just a few years ago. You may be far less mobile than you were before you required a walker or wheelchair. Then there's your cognition. You may be a bit more forgetful than you've been in the past, not remembering where you placed your smart phone or if you took your medications this morning. For dementia patients, not remembering even if they have eaten their previous meal can be an issue.

During our No-Go Years, we may require assisted care one or two days a week or twenty-four hours a day, seven days a week in one of the care facilities you read about previously. Also, your diminished physical state or mental state or both may require you, as Natalie's story about her mother demonstrated, to give up your car keys. This is particularly a difficult realty for many who have associated driving their cars with their independence. But as far as this is concerned, the future appears bright. Current technology has given us more options than ever. Uber, Lyft, and other ride-sharing platforms have provided both young and old alike unprecedented degrees of mobility. And with autonomous cars hitting the mainstream over the next few years, for elderly and handicapped people, the experience of being forced to forfeit their keys or, even worse, being ineligible to obtain a driver's license, may go the way of the horse and buggy.

The following is a sample of insights respondents provided me that relate to the No-Go Years. Note that rather than their own views, they are reflecting what they've heard expressed from elderly parents, family members, and friends who were at this stage of life. In the first part, you'll read what the elderly person actually said. Next, the part in parentheses reflects reality:

- You have taken all my money! (The family member did this once the parent entered a care facility, where carrying money was not necessary. From cash in a purse to bank accounts, over time the parent thought all her money was taken away, which wasn't the case.)

- You've left me with nothing! (This person in the No-Go Years said this while in his home because he no longer recognized his furniture and possessions. He couldn't even identify who was in the family photos anymore.)

- You haven't been here in weeks. (The family member had visited the day before.)

- I hate this place! YOU put me here! (This woman was placing guilt on the family member who took her to the new facility. Despite her complaint, she was participating in many of the activities being offered in the care facility, and the staff indicated that she was mostly a happy person.)

- I love it here! I just wish Mom would visit. (This person was referring to his deceased parent who had passed away thirty years ago.)

- The food here is terrible! There's nothing for me to eat. (This, despite the fact the person had gained twenty pounds over the last year while dining on this supposedly terrible food.)

Lastly, a story from a client:

We had to move Dad to another facility because, despite his dementia, he became enamored with a resident while his wife was also in the same place. He no longer recognized his wife, but she recognized him and became very agitated!

Do any of these insights resonate with you?

If you've been planning for this stage (for instance, you've implemented the processes I've described throughout this book), then you are entering the No-Go Years with everything in order and you're still in control of your life to the greatest extent possible. And, as the advent of autonomous cars demonstrates, in a few years you'll have unprecedented options that will further improve your quality of life.

CARE OPTIONS: SKILLED NURSING CARE FACILITIES

When your individual needs fall outside the scope of the facilities described in the Go-Go and Slow-Go Years (adult-only and senior-only care, assisted living, and memory care facilities), a nursing home is often the next step. Keep in mind, a CCRC may have a nursing home option as well. In this case, patients do not have to be moved away from the current facility, and if their spouse is living, then they will easily be able to see each other.

Generally, nursing homes come into play when you're unable to care for yourself due to mental or physical impairments or your health status is considered terminal. Because nursing home care is much more intensive and requires a full-time professional staff, its costs can be dramatically higher than what you've been paying for your current level of care.

There is a big misconception that you can qualify for nursing home care under Medicare or Medicaid. While under certain circumstances this may be the case, you'll have to meet stringent requirements to qualify. Medicare will provide short-term rehabilitation type of care, such as recovering from surgery. But it does not provide long-term care.

In order to qualify for nursing home care under Medicaid, you must exhaust nearly all your assets. In addition, because Medicaid is intended to help those with limited or no financial resources, you may need to fall under certain federal categories such as requiring federally assisted income benefits. And after all this, if your nursing home care is covered, you're only allowed to live in Medicaid-qualified facilities. Because Medicaid is run by the individual states and not the federal government, the Medicaid bed you are eligible to stay in may be located in a different community from where you currently live. If you're uncertain about your eligibility, an elder law attorney can help you obtain the benefits you're entitled to under the current laws of your state.

PAYING FOR CARE SERVICES WHEN RESOURCES ARE LIMITED

What if you're ineligible to have your long-term care costs covered under Medicaid, your LTC policy doesn't provide enough coverage, or you don't have LTC at all? Are you destined to live out the rest of your life in poverty? Or, as many of my female clients have told me over the years, "Stan, my biggest fear is becoming a bag lady!" And keep in mind this worry often comes from people who are in financially solid shape, which points to how widespread the anxiety is of outliving one's savings. Let's explore alternative options that can provide additional resources during the No-Go Years.

Whole life insurance policies: if you were fortunate enough to have purchased a permanent life insurance plan (whole life, universal life, or variable life), then you most likely have several options to access the accumulated cash values. All you need to do is make withdrawals or take loans from the policy to provide you the additional cash you need. This provides tax-free access to the cash value, but it may reduce the death benefit depending upon the type of policy you have.

Certain types of care you require or terminal illnesses can also qualify you to access your life insurance policy's cash value or even early death benefits. For this to work, you needed to have set up the policy while younger in order to build up the cash value. Or you may be able to convert an existing permanent policy, under a tax-free exchange, into a newer life insurance policy that has LTC benefits as well as terminal-illness benefits.

A life settlement: this allows you to generate a lump sum payment by selling your existing life, whole life, or term life insurance policy for an amount that is greater than the accumulated cash value but less than the death benefit. Once you receive the settlement amount, you can then use it to reduce debt or pay for needed care.

A life settlement is done via the secondary life insurance market where you sell your life insurance policy to a third party. This works whether you own term or whole life insurance, and the amount you receive is determined by your recalculated life expectancy (LE), which is a process that analyzes your present health. Typically, the third-party buyer will be looking for a person with a calculated LE of less than five years.

Life settlement companies will buy a person's life insurance policy and continue to pay the premiums. Upon your death, the company will obtain the death benefit. There are many factors in this process that will determine the amount of the payment to the owner of the policy, so performing a cost-benefit analysis is important.

The advantage of a life settlement is you will receive cash as soon as possible to pay for your expenses. The disadvantage is your beneficiaries will not receive your life insurance death benefit. Life settlements may be an option for those unfortunate individuals who have no other financial resources and want to avoid becoming dependent upon family, friends, or charity or do not want to burden their surviving families with the medical bills that have accumulated.

Keep in mind this is not a viatical settlement, which is an arrangement where companies buy policies from people with a terminal illness and have a LE of less than a year, rather than the life settlement's five years or less LE. Viatical settlements are controversial because some providers of life settlements used predatory tactics to take advantage of people who were on their deathbeds.

A reverse mortgage: with a reverse mortgage, you are able to tap into your home equity without creating another debt that requires monthly payments. This works for those who own their home and have a small mortgage balance or no mortgage, and when the total amount of monthly income the reverse mortgage provides you does not exceed half the residence's value. At some point, the house will be sold, and the bank will recoup the amount it paid you through the reverse mortgage arrangement. This is a good option for those with limited liquid resources who want to stay in their homes for as long as possible during their retirement.

The biggest advantage of a reverse mortgage is that you are not forced to sell your home in order to have access to its equity. Also, qualifying for a reverse mortgage is often a simpler process than qualifying for a regular mortgage. The disadvantage is that you are reducing the remaining value of the property for heirs or yourself if you live too long and then have to sell the property to utilize the remainder of the equity. Also, you're required to continue paying to maintain the property, the real estate taxes, and homeowner's insurance.

NOTE: *If you sell your home after having a reverse mortgage, the accumulated interest that is then paid to the lender becomes deductible in the year of the sale.*

LTC AND ACCELERATED DEATH BENEFIT RIDERS

Your life insurance policy may have a no-cost accelerated death benefit rider. This allows you to take advances on your death benefit if you meet certain requirements; the one most frequently used is a terminal illness diagnosis that leaves you with an LE of less than a year.

LTC and accelerated death benefit riders came about as a way to deter the dark players in the viatical business from preying on the most vulnerable. Next, some life insurance policies and annuity products provide LTC benefits that are built into the contract itself and provide specified amounts of LTC benefits at the time of need. Here again, you may be able to acquire a policy with these benefits while in the earlier stages of retirement and before you have major health issues. You may also have the option to convert an existing policy to one that has these benefit options, or riders.

The main advantage of these two riders on life insurance and annuity policies is they will allow you to receive the care you need by providing funds that can reduce the likelihood you'll go into debt. The only negative is that the amount of benefits paid out of these policies will reduce their remaining value to your beneficiaries.

In the next section, we'll explore the pitfalls that exist in the Slow-Go Years through the experiences of a couple, Peter and Karen.

DETERMINING CARE OPTIONS AFTER PROCRASTINATION

Peter and Karen, a couple in their eighties, thought they had done their part to plan for their retirement. They had prepared an estate plan in order to avoid probate, and they had taken care of many items on the abbreviated checklist in chapter 3 (see the full list in appendix A).

Unfortunately, they neglected to give much thought to their care options. Rather than answer tough questions about what they would do if they could no longer age in place well, they stuck with the status quo because it was comfortable: Their one-story house meant they had no stairs to deal with and made navigating from one part of the home to the other easy. They lived near family and their golf club, where they spent hours with friends. Thinking beyond their pleasant quality of life seemed unnecessary and downright depressing.

The status quo went smoothly until Peter gradually began losing his memory and was eventually diagnosed with dementia. Once his condition was identified, his cognition quickly deteriorated. His care needs soon exceeded what Karen could physically manage on her own, and she realized he needed significant professional help. As a result, she hired 24-7 homecare services that included a nurse and cook because Karen's own physical state reached a point where she struggled preparing meals for both of them throughout the day.

The more Peter's dementia worsened, the more Karen felt isolated at home because she could no longer communicate with her husband the way she used to. At the same time, as her friends advanced in age, they began moving to live closer to their own families, and this chipped away at her prized social circle.

To Karen's great regret, they had not purchased an LTC policy before their transition into retirement, and doing so now was impossible because they could no longer qualify due to their ages and current medical condition. Unfortunately, no LTC policies cover pre-existing conditions. The only revenue sources the couple had were their retirement accounts and Social Security. With Peter's expensive homecare rapidly depleting the couple's nest egg, Karen began having heightened anxiety. Worries about not having enough money to pay for her husband's care, and even greater fears about not having any funds left for her once he passed, kept her up at night.

Karen was a proud mother and didn't want to disclose her dilemma to her adult children—the last thing she wanted was to be a burden to them. But with her concerns about becoming insolvent and uncertainty as to how to take care of Peter as his health continued going downhill, she reached out to them for help.

With the support and input of her two kids, Karen made the difficult decision to move Peter into a local care facility's memory care unit. Her children found one that also provided assisted care, which would allow Karen and Peter to live in the same facility.

With the help of their children, Karen was able to determine which household items to keep and which to give away or donate. With this step out of the way, they sold their home. The sale's net proceeds were sufficient to rebuild their liquid resources, so Karen could reduce her anxiety about running out of money. She no longer had to maintain the house, she had her living needs taken care of, and she could maintain constant contact with her husband.

The downside of this plan was its cost. By the time Peter and Karen passed, they had spent down the majority of their assets. While their estate documents had included covering their grandchildren's college tuition, there was no money left to do so. Previously, their adult children had counted on their parents' help to pay for the grandkids' college costs. They were disappointed when they realized this wouldn't be possible. At the same time, when Karen had initially broken the bad news about her financially compromised state, her kids knew the college funds wouldn't be there, and this gave them time to develop a plan B.

While Peter's dementia and its cost abruptly derailed the couple's retirement plan, their situation could have been far worse if they hadn't built up a large nest egg prior to their retirement. Also, the equity in their home provided a significant funding source to cover their care facility costs. Had they depleted all their money, this would have forced them to enroll in Medicaid.

In order to avoid what Peter and Karen went through, having LTC insurance is imperative. Also, a Real Retirement Plan would have considered the dementia scenario that the couple neglected to address. Last, maintaining as much freedom and independence as possible during the No-Go Years requires regularly reviewing your retirement plan with your spouse and family members.

LIVING WELL DURING YOUR NO-GO YEARS

During this stage of life, many people experience various degrees of incapacitation. Therefore, they may be in a care facility and unable to perform many of the activities that were part of normal life in the past—from simple daily tasks such as feeding and walking the dog to working out at the gym. While this is cause for some to plunge into depression, despondency doesn't have to be your destiny.

I've known my share of men and women who went downhill emotionally once they reached the No-Go Years and were basically waiting to die. But I've also known plenty of people who lived well under otherwise adverse circumstances. Your mindset matters. A positive outlook that is open to change will put you in a place to see possibility rather than limitations. For instance, your body may be too frail for you to walk on your own, but walkers and wheelchairs can help many in the No-Go Years get around. In addition, medical advances are providing options for mobility and wellbeing that didn't exist just a generation ago.

Staying engaged is key as well. Family and friends provide those in the No-Go Years with social bonds that keep a person connected with his or her community. Participating in activities is another important way to provide consistent mental stimulation.

For family members and friends of those in the No-Go Years, these are challenging times as well. The person may seem unable to fully grasp who is visiting or why. Thus, your presence may seem unnecessary. But my take on this is that your presence does matter. Regardless of how much the other person recognizes you, you certainly know and care about who this special person is.

HINT: *Avoiding procrastination and planning for the mental and physical limitations that you'll most likely experience during the No-Go Years is key to increasing the likelihood that you'll maintain a level of care that aligns with your expectations as well as your budget.*

CHAPTER 13

THE EXIT

I have to write down what I've experienced taking care of Mom, so I won't have to go through what she did if I have to enter a care facility.

- Survey respondent

BOTH MY PROFESSIONAL AND personal experiences have taught me that most people do not apply the same attention to detail to planning their retirement years as they did in order to get them to retirement itself. This lack of planning often has to do with fear—fear of thinking about dying and living life in a nursing home or memory care facility leads to procrastination. However, the reality is that just the opposite happens when planning your retirement years. You reduce or eliminate your fears and anxieties and establish a plan to take care of you right up to the end. In addition, you give your surviving family members peace of mind because they know they're acting in a way that ensures your wishes are being carried out.

When Marta was a child, she would wake up in the morning and need a couple of minutes to make sense of her surroundings as she transitioned from her dream to the waking state. Once she recognized the objects around her, the world made sense, and she'd continue with the habits and patterns she'd relied on for years.

Now that Marta was on the other end of her lifespan, she found herself in a similar hazy place every morning that she had experienced in her youth. But unlike the fog that lifted after a few minutes when she was a child, it remained thick and impenetrable throughout the day. It clouded her ability to make sense of the world around her and essentially served as a border between her and reality.

In her disoriented state, simple tasks, such as picking out an outfit to wear, felt like being charged to solve the world's thorniest math problem. She was bombarded with memories amassed over decades of living that served to add another layer of distraction that further derailed her ability to interpret the present. People would come visit her, and they called her Mom, Grandma, Auntie, and Marta, and she struggled to decipher the words or the faces behind them.

From receiving help going to the bathroom to family members that felt like strangers visiting her, Marta's world felt out of control, which would sometimes cause her to become angry. *Who are these people? What are they doing to me? What are they saying?* Marta felt trapped in a ceaseless state of confusion. Sometimes her despondency would cause her to declare, "I'm jumping out the window!"

No doubt, Marta and those charged to care for her were all drowning under the responsibility of meeting her needs.

DEALING WITH THE FINAL STAGES OF LIFE

If you have had to care for aging parents, then you know it can be incredibly stressful having to make difficult decisions about the level of care, coordinating the care, paying the bills, and trying to maintain a good relationship with them. This is made more difficult if your parents have a form of dementia to the point that they may not understand why you are doing what you are doing to help them, they may express anger and often make accusations about your having stolen all their money, or they may tell you they no longer have a life worth living and wish they were dead. They may even make threats that they will jump out the window. It is hard to imagine what they are going through: no longer able to understand what is happening in their world, having only glimpses of their past, and not being able to make decisions for things as simple as what to wear when they get up in the morning.

For others it is not the dementia but the diagnosis of a terminal illness or debilitating disease or reoccurrence of a cancer they thought they had beat, only to discover it in a completely different location. As the old expression states, "There are only two certainties in life: taxes and death!" Dealing with the taxes is the easy part; making plans for our demise is the most difficult task and maybe the most important one we can ever take on.

The following is a sample of insights respondents provided me that relate to the Exit. Note that in addition to their own views, some of the following reflect what they've heard expressed from elderly parents, other family members, and friends who were at this stage of life:

- I don't understand how she is still living.

- Why can't the doctors just give him more pain pills to relieve his pain?

- After taking care of them, arranging their care, and managing their financials, I just know that I do not want to place that burden on our kids.

- We were lucky. Our parents did enter a continuing care facility early enough so that they formed new friendships and were able to live out their lives in security and being well taken care of.

- This is all happening at the time when my adult kids are building families of their own and moving away for new job opportunities. I cannot join them until Mom passes, and she is so ornery that she may just live to one hundred!

- I did not know about all of their assets and liabilities until they died, and I found out that I was the executor and successor trustee. My siblings were not happy with that choice!

Do any of these insights resonate with you?

Let's look at some of the issues at this stage and see how best to prepare for them, everything from a good up-to-date estate plan to writing a family love letter.

This is really about how you can help your parents as well as yourself to prepare for declining capacity and end-of-life issues. It is time to stop and think about what they really want and not what you think they want based upon your own feelings. In many instances, when there are multiple siblings involved with the care of aging parents, emotions run high as each has a different perspective regarding what is the right thing to do for their parents' care.

So here is my first rule when dealing with this stage: get professional guidance. And do this before your parents or you become unable to make those decisions. That means having the discussion early in the Go-Go Years and following up with annual family meetings, reviewing the estate documents at least every five years, and having your parents write down what is most important to them as they age. If not done previously, this is also a good time for parents to write a family love letter that tells the children and grandchildren what some of their best memories were and how they wish to be remembered when they are gone.

MANAGING WITHOUT LTC INSURANCE

Carol's husband died at age eighty. At the time of his passing, she was in good health and living in the house they'd called home for the past twenty years. The couple had purchased it before retirement and built the house in a golf community near the nineteenth hole. They enjoyed the country club lifestyle, made many friends, and participated in many tournaments and activities at the golf club.

However, two years after her husband had died, Carol's memory began to fail, and she required assistance with activities from transportation to managing her bills. Unfortunately, Carol refused to acknowledge her deteriorating condition or obtain any help in her home, other than a cleaning lady who came once a week. Although she was clearly a hazard on the road, she would not stop driving.

After six months of persuasion, her friends and family finally convinced Carol to give up her car keys, admit she could no longer live safely on her own, and move to a CCRC. Her new home would be close to her friends and family, so she would be able to see them often.

At the same time, Carol was eighty-two, and she was concerned about running money out of money—particularly because she didn't have LTC insurance. This is a common concern for people in memory care because they lose their ability to understand financial matters. This may lead them to think they have no money, even when they may have enough to provide for all their needs. Fortunately, for Carol and her family, she had sufficient savings and investments from the sale of her house, the survivor benefits from her husband's pension, and Social Security retirement benefits.

Combined, these gave her the income she needed to cover her growing expenses, and she was able to live out her life and leave a small financial legacy to her children.

For many others who do not have significant liquid assets, the likelihood of running out of money is a legitimate concern and the primary reason for having an LTC insurance policy. No one wants to make the choice of providing the necessary care for their parents versus having them live out their lives in an undesirable environment. This may also affect the next generation, as many will end up contributing to the cost of care to keep their parent in a place that will provide the needed quality care and not just in a Medicaid bed.

NOTE: *If your parents are under age seventy-five and on a tight budget, consider buying LTC insurance for them. This will be much less expensive then helping them pay for care at the time of an incapacity.*

CARE OPTION: HOSPICE

This is a specific type of palliative care for people who likely have six months or less to live. It is designed to give compassionate and supportive care to people in the last stages of a serious illness, such as cancer or heart failure. Hospice focuses on comfort and quality of life, rather than providing cures. Its goal is to enable patients to be comfortable and pain free, so they live each day as fully as possible. Note that hospice does not charge the patient for these services; it does get reimbursements from Medicare and is funded by private donations.

Hospice provides care services, emotional support, and spiritual resources for people in this stage, as well as assistance to family or friends or both as they face this difficult time. Some hospice care providers may be medically trained. Meanwhile, other hospice care providers are volunteers who are there to assist and be a companion to the patient as he or she lives out the final days of life.

Hospice care also helps family members manage the practical details and emotional challenges of caring for a dying loved one. This includes providing information on what to expect as patients near their end of life, as well as following up after the death by providing grief-counseling resources.

The way hospice care is administered varies depending on the patient's needs and financial resources. Patients may be in their own home and receive services from hospice, in a hospice care facility, or in a non-hospice care facility receiving hospice services. In regard to the latter, this means patients may be living in a nursing facility or long-term care facility and receive specialized visits from hospice nurses, home health aides, chaplains, social workers, and volunteers. These services are in addition to other previous and ongoing services provided by the care facility.

Note that only medical professionals are authorized to administer prescription medications with one exception. In the case of home hospice care, family members may be allowed to administer medications when a hospice nurse is not available.

After the patient dies, the hospice personnel will assist in transferring the deceased to a mortuary and notifying the patient's doctor because doctors, not a hospice nurse, are charged to sign the death certificate.

Throughout my life, I have dealt with both my own family members' end-of-life issues and those of my clients. In all cases, where hospice was involved, the level of care for both the patient and the family has been extraordinary. Hospice care professionals are well trained in all aspects of this end-of-life process and should be seen as angels in our midst!

LIVING WELL, RIGHT UP TO THE END

As my priest has told me, "Be prepared because we never know when God will want us to join him in heaven." No doubt, our end of life could come at any time. In fact, research has shown us that 100 percent of the people in our world today will die. So, if death is inevitable, why not plan for it as you would have done or are doing for your retirement? I've told some of my clients how I was amazed that they spent more time planning their vacations than planning for their financial wellness! Part of the issue is that many people are all in denial—especially baby boomers. I'm always amazed how many of them act as if they will be the first person to not die!

The purpose of a Real Retirement Plan is to allow you to have the best quality of life possible as you age while at the same time preparing your family to carry out what you truly wish for the end-of-your-life story. A Real Retirement Plan will both save you a great deal of money in the long term and reduce the emotional burden your family, friends, and all those you would like to benefit from your estate will experience upon your passing. By following the recommendations I've provided in this book, you have the information you need to leave a lasting legacy that represents your values and the love you have for those closest to you.

**It is not what you gather but what you scatter
that tells what kind of life you have lived.**
– ANONYMOUS

REAL RETIREMENT PLAN CHECKLIST

THE FOLLOWING IS A list of questions for you to answer and discuss with your partner and possibly your children. By addressing each of these questions, you'll identify the key elements necessary to have your one best retirement life.

If you do respond positively to a question, then also be sure that other family members are aware of where items are located or where to find important documents or even the updated list of passwords. As discussed in the book, be sure to include your executor or successor trustee and your attorney in fact for the power of attorney and medical directives.

1. Have you updated your financial statement in the past year? It should include bank account balances; retirement plan values; and changes in mortgage balance, student loans, credit card balances, or any other values of assets.

2. Have you updated your estate documents in the past five years? Documents like POAs and medical directives may

have a shelf life that would make them unusable after a certain period. Estate and income tax laws are constantly changing. As your family or financial situations change, all the estate documents should be updated.

3. The court of wills requires you to have an original will in order to establish the probate estate and to be recognized as the executor. Do you know where your original estate documents are stored? Does your executor or successor trustee know where they are?

4. Do you know specifically what your will and trust state for the distribution of assets?

5. Are your executor and successor trustee aware of their roles in your estate plan?

6. Have you documented what you want to happen to your personal belongings after you pass?

7. Do you have an updated list of all credit cards that can be accessed easily in order to keep your payments up to date? Information about the cards should also state who obtained the credit cards and whose names are included for each. Note: If you are handling the affairs of one who has died, make sure you destroy the deceased person's credit cards.

8. Have you obtained a credit report from the major credit bureaus this year?

9. Have you enrolled in a credit and identity-theft monitoring system such as LifeLock?

10. Do you know what the death benefits are on your life insurance policies and what type of life insurance you have? If term life, do you know when it expires?

11. Do you know the beneficiaries named on all life insurance policies and retirement accounts?

12. Have you identified the contingent beneficiaries in your insurance policies and retirement plans?

13. Do you understand what your liability, property, and casualty insurance coverage limitations are? Have you updated these policies in the past three years?

14. Do you know where all the original documents are for the purchase of the family home and investment statements?

15. Do you have a list of account websites and passwords that can easily be accessed by your family?

16. Do you have a key to the bank safe deposit box or the key or combination to the in-house safe that can be easily accessed in the event you're incapacitated or pass?

17. Do you have the contact information for professional advisers such as your attorney, insurance agent, financial planner, accountant, and family doctor?

18. Have you designated who will be responsible for your care in the event you're incapacitated, and is this person aware of his or her responsibility?

19. Have you made plans to pay for the cost of care or for how to finance the cost of care?

20. Do you have a list of your monthly bills that need to be paid so someone can take care of them for you in the event you're incapacitated? Note: Consider enrolling in automatic payments or online bill pay.

21. If you own a business and you are still the rainmaker, do you have a succession plan in place?

22. Have you determined if you would like to make family gifts during your lifetime?

23. Do you have a list of charities you wish to benefit from your estate?

24. Have you written a memorandum or letter of instruction to be attached to your will or trust that provides guidance as to what specific personal items you wish to go to certain family members?

25. Have you shared your family history with future generations, perhaps through a family meeting?

26. Have you planned your funeral, chosen the burial plot, and established the type of service you want?

EXECUTOR DUTIES AND RESPONSIBILITIES

- Find the latest will and read it.

- Obtain permission from the court to represent the estate of the decedent. This is called a "letter of testimony" in some jurisdictions or a "letter of appointment" in others.

- File a petition with the court to probate the will.

- Assemble all the decedent's assets.

- Take possession of safe deposit box contents.

- Consult with banks and savings and loans to find all accounts of the deceased.

- Check for cash and other valuables hidden around the home.

- Transfer all securities to the executor's name and continue to collect dividends and interest on behalf of the heirs of the deceased.

- Locate information on life insurance and any other insurance policies including auto, home, LTC, umbrella, and health. Identify all named beneficiaries of insurance policies, retirement plans, and any other assets with a designated beneficiary.

- Inventory all the personal possessions and tangible personal property, including cars, boats, and household items.

- Collect all life insurance proceeds payable to the estate.

- Obtain copies of all real estate deeds, mortgages, leases, and tax information.

- Apply for benefits under the various group and individual plans of the decedent.

- Obtain a tax identification number and collect all the investment assets under the name of the estate.

- Obtain immediate management for rental properties.

- Locate any property or assets held in other states. Then arrange ancillary administration for out-of-state property.

- Collect monies owed to the deceased.

- Obtain appraisals of any real property and valuable artifacts.

- Determine liquidity needs.

- Maintain bookkeeping records of every amount that came into the estate and that was paid out of the estate.

- Review the investment portfolio.

- Sell appropriate assets.

- Pay valid claims against the estate, reject improper claims, and defend the estate if necessary.

- Pay all debts of the estate, including final expenses and any other debts from time of death.

- Pay state and federal taxes due.

- File income tax returns for the decedent and the estate.

- Determine whether the estate qualifies for special use valuation under IRS section 2032A or the deferral of estate taxes under IRS sections 6161 or 6166.

- If the surviving spouse isn't a US citizen, consider a qualified domestic trust to defer the payment of federal estate taxes.

- File a federal estate tax return. File a state tax death tax return or state inheritance tax return or both.

- Prepare statements of all receipts and disbursements.

- Pay attorney's fees and executor's commissions.

- Assist the attorney in defending the estate if necessary.

- Notify the beneficiaries and make distributions to them on a timely basis.

- Distribute specific bequests and the remainder of the decedent's assets.

- Provide the required court filings for probate and a final accounting to close the estate.

- Obtain tax releases and receipts as directed by the court.

- Establish a testamentary trust (or pour over into a living trust) when appropriate.

IRS LIFE EXPECTANCY TABLE FOR DETERMINING RMDs

Reference the Internal Revenue Service document, "Publication 590-B: Distributions from Individual Retirement Arrangements (IRAs)," which will provide details regarding the rules for the IRA required minimum distributions. You can find it on the IRS website, **www.irs.gov**, and search for Publication 590-B.

UNIFORM LIFETIME TABLE
IRS Reg. 1.401(a)(9)-9

Age	Distribution	Age	Distribution
70	27.4	93	9.6
71	26.5	94	9.1
72	25.6	95	8.6
73	24.7	96	8.1
74	23.8	97	7.6
75	22.9	98	7.1
76	22.0	99	6.7
77	21.2	100	6.3
78	20.3	101	5.9
79	19.5	102	5.5
80	18.7	103	5.2
81	17.9	104	4.9
82	17.1	105	4.5
83	16.3	106	4.2
84	15.5	107	3.9
85	14.8	108	3.7
86	14.1	109	3.4
87	13.4	110	3.1
88	12.7	111	2.9
89	12.0	112	2.6
90	11.4	113	2.4
91	10.8	114	2.1
92	10.2	115 and over	1.9

Source: IRS Required Minimum Distribution Worksheet, Table III (Uniform Lifetime)

THE RETIREMENT EXPECTATIONS EXERCISE

NSWER THE FOLLOWING QUESTIONS, and if you have a significant other, have that person also create his or her own responses:

- What are your vision and your personal expectations in retirement?

- What is on your bucket list?

- What are your biggest concerns for this period of your life?

- What activities have you talked about doing but never found the time to do before while working?

- Have you thought about relocating? If so, where?

- How comfortable are you managing your finances?

- If you were lying on your deathbed, what would you regret not having done?

- Can you identify what is most important to you at this stage of your life?

- What is the plan for the ultimate disposition of your assets?

- Will having grandchildren influence any of the preceding answers?

- If you are partnered, are you each aligned with the expectations, goals, and wishes of the other?

Once you've answered your questions individually, share them with each other and compare. Did you both have the same expectations about retirement? Identify and discuss where you have common interests and ones that aren't aligned. By both of you expressing your feelings, you'll be able to make decisions together going forward that reflect both of your perspectives.

ACKNOWLEDGEMENTS

I **WANT TO THANK** all former and current clients as each had a role in helping me be a better professional advisor. And a special thanks to all of those who took the time to complete the questionnaire I sent out to gain greater insight, guidance, and inspiration into how they were dealing with the different stages of their own retirement.

Special thanks go to several individuals who have assisted me with some of the technical, legal, emotional, and HR issues addressed in this book.

Angela Watson, retired HR director
Elizabeth Gray, attorney, McCandlish Lillard Law
Jerry Grossman, retired corporate executive
Bill Smith, corporate executive
Rick Knop, entrepreneur
Bizu Hodge, marketing manager
Mark Decker, retired attorney and corporate executive
Lewis Schumann, semi-retired attorney
Dr. Michael Arons, psychiatrist
Lawrence Ineno, editor
Colleen Orme, marketing professional
Jayme Juncker, my wife and the love of my life

ABOUT THE AUTHOR

 **STAN COREY** has been a Certified Financial Planner (CFP) Professional, Chartered Financial Consultant (ChFC), and Certified Private Wealth Advisor (CPWA) and has worked with many individuals, families, and small businesses for almost forty years. He has retired from the day-to-day activity of providing financial advisory services but continues to consult in specialized areas, such as assisting clients with estate settlements, a financial advocate in divorce cases working with family law attorneys, and speaking at various professional conferences, and plans to continue writing about current financial issues.

Stan was born in New York City and grew up in Stony Brook on Long Island. After graduating from American International College in Springfield, Massachusetts, in 1971, he joined the navy and was stationed at Bethesda National Naval Medical Center and Patuxent Naval Air Station hospital, both in Maryland. Although he never served on a ship, since childhood, Stan has been an avid sailor, and navigating the seas has been his lifelong passion. He has sailed most of the East Coast, as well as to Bermuda. For over twenty years, he competed in numerous sailing club and international regattas as skipper, helmsman, and tactician on a variety of boats from fifteen feet to sixty feet. He won the Naval District of Washington sailing championship in 1974 and became an ocean racing coach for the Naval Academy after his honorable discharge in 1976.

Stan is a sought-after financial expert who regularly provides commentary at national conferences, in print and online publications, and on TV. He is author of a teaching novel, *The Divorce Dance*. He has appeared in *USA Today*, *Working Women* magazine, *MONEY*, *Good Housekeeping*, and *Northern Virginia* magazine and is a regular contributor to a women's retirement blog, *Sixty and Me*. For twenty years, he published the *News and Views*, a quarterly newsletter covering financial topics; and he co-wrote and taught the Economic Issues in Divorce curriculum, which is a required course for mediator certification through Northern Virginia Mediation Services (NVMS). Stan works closely with foremost family law firms in Northern Virginia providing financial expertise and serves as an expert witness and financial advocate for the financially less well informed. As a "financial translator," he has earned a reputation for taking complex financial issues and making them understandable to non-experts.

Stan currently lives in Great Falls, Virginia, with his wife, Jayme. When they're not spending time with their adult children and grandchildren, the couple enjoys traveling, golfing, and an occasional sail with old friends.

Made in the USA
Middletown, DE
18 October 2018